SELF-LEARNING MANAGEMENT SERIES

DIVERSITY IN THE WORKPLACE ESSENTIALS
YOU ALWAYS WANTED TO KNOW

A multi-perspective view of diversity and inclusion in the 21st-century workplace.

JAQUINA GILBERT

Diversity in the Workplace
Essentials You Always Wanted To Know
First Edition

© 2022, By Vibrant Publishers, USA. All rights reserved. No part of this publication may be reproduced or distributed in any form or by any means, or stored in a database or retrieval system, without the prior permission of the publisher.

Paperback ISBN 10: 1-63651-112-0
Paperback ISBN 13: 978-1-63651-112-2

Ebook ISBN 10: 1-63651-113-9
Ebook ISBN 13: 978-1-63651-113-9

Hardback ISBN 10: 1-63651-114-7
Hardback ISBN 13: 978-1-63651-114-6

Library of Congress Control Number: 2022936608

This publication is designed to provide accurate and authoritative information in regard to the subject matter covered. The Author has made every effort in the preparation of this book to ensure the accuracy of the information. However, information in this book is sold without warranty either expressed or implied. The Author or the Publisher will not be liable for any damages caused or alleged to be caused either directly or indirectly by this book.

Vibrant Publishers books are available at special quantity discount for sales promotions, or for use in corporate training programs. For more information please write to bulkorders@vibrantpublishers.com

Please email feedback / corrections (technical, grammatical or spelling) to spellerrors@vibrantpublishers.com

To access the complete catalogue of Vibrant Publishers, visit www.vibrantpublishers.com

SELF-LEARNING MANAGEMENT SERIES

TITLE	PAPERBACK* ISBN
ACCOUNTING, FINANCE & ECONOMICS	
COST ACCOUNTING AND MANAGEMENT ESSENTIALS	9781636511030
FINANCIAL ACCOUNTING ESSENTIALS	9781636510972
FINANCIAL MANAGEMENT ESSENTIALS	9781636511009
MACROECONOMICS ESSENTIALS	9781636511818
MICROECONOMICS ESSENTIALS	9781636511153
PERSONAL FINANCE ESSENTIALS	9781636511849
ENTREPRENEURSHIP & STRATEGY	
BUSINESS PLAN ESSENTIALS	9781636511214
BUSINESS STRATEGY ESSENTIALS	9781949395778
ENTREPRENEURSHIP ESSENTIALS	9781636511603
GENERAL MANAGEMENT	
BUSINESS LAW ESSENTIALS	9781636511702
DECISION MAKING ESSENTIALS	9781636510026
LEADERSHIP ESSENTIALS	9781636510316
PRINCIPLES OF MANAGEMENT ESSENTIALS	9781636511542
TIME MANAGEMENT ESSENTIALS	9781636511665

*Also available in Hardback & Ebook formats

SELF-LEARNING MANAGEMENT SERIES

TITLE	PAPERBACK* ISBN
HUMAN RESOURCE MANAGEMENT	
DIVERSITY IN THE WORKPLACE ESSENTIALS	9781636511122
HR ANALYTICS ESSENTIALS	9781636510347
HUMAN RESOURCE MANAGEMENT ESSENTIALS	9781949395839
ORGANIZATIONAL BEHAVIOR ESSENTIALS	9781636510378
ORGANIZATIONAL DEVELOPMENT ESSENTIALS	9781636511481
MARKETING & SALES MANAGEMENT	
DIGITAL MARKETING ESSENTIALS	9781949395747
MARKETING MANAGEMENT ESSENTIALS	9781636511788
SALES MANAGEMENT ESSENTIALS	9781636510743
SERVICES MARKETING ESSENTIALS	9781636511733
OPERATIONS & PROJECT MANAGEMENT	
AGILE ESSENTIALS	9781636510057
OPERATIONS & SUPPLY CHAIN MANAGEMENT ESSENTIALS	9781949395242
PROJECT MANAGEMENT ESSENTIALS	9781636510712
STAKEHOLDER ENGAGEMENT ESSENTIALS	9781636511511

*Also available in Hardback & Ebook formats

About the Author

Jaquina Gilbert has over 20 years of experience in Human Resources in multiple disciplines and holds SHRM and PHR certifications. She has authored several books, developed professional certification test material, and written HR-related articles, manuals, and training content for other professionals in various industries. Jaquina received a BBA in Human Resources Management and Organizational Behavior from the University of North Texas in Denton and an MS in Human Resources Training and Development from Amberton University.

Other contributors

We would like to thank our editor, Franca Roibal Fernandez for her contribution to making this book the best version possible. She is Visiting Assistant Professor of Spanish Modern Languages & Literatures at Moravian University, a DEI Practitioner, and a Social Justice Advocate.

What experts say about this book!

This is a book that encompasses a lot of key information in an accessible way. The points are organized well. The values of diversity are clearly expressed, with a detailed explanation of its history and background. I recommend this book for school libraries as a faculty reference material and for students' research projects. The context is well thought through and accessible to people belonging to different groups.

**– Abby Ahlers, Librarian/Media Specialist,
Village Christian School**

The topic is fascinating and a crucial issue in HRM these days. The chapters are written in an orderly manner. Everything looks good to me.

**– Fariba Azizzadeh, Ph.D, Assistant Professor,
Islamic Azad University**

Diversity in the Workplace Essentials You Always Wanted to Know is a great and in-depth book showing a step-by-step view how leaders must sincerely value a variety of opinions, and how organizational culture must encourage openness and make workers feel valued. For any organization that is looking to understand how Diversity in the Workplace looks and feels, I highly recommend this once in a lifetime book gem.

**– Dr. Denean Robinson, Adjunct Faculty Member,
University of Maryland Baltimore County**

This page is intentionally left blank

Table of Contents

1 Identity — 1
1.1 Historical Background of Identity and Diversity   9
1.2 Privilege and White Fragility   16
1.3 Intersectionality   27
1.4 Multiculturalism   31
Quiz   33
Chapter Summary   36

2 Diversity — 39
2.1 Physical Appearance and Attributes   41
2.2 Physical and Mental Abilities   43
2.3 Sex and Gender   44
2.4 Age   48
2.5 Race, Ethnicity and Nationality   51
2.6 Status   58
2.7 Language and Communication   61
2.8 Spirituality and Religion   65
2.9 Socioeconomic Background   66
2.10 Learning Style   67
2.11 Working Style   70
2.12 Talents, Skills, and Aptitude   72
Quiz   75
Chapter Summary   78

3 Organizational Culture — 81
3.1 Impact of Diversity on Organizational Culture   87
3.2 Harassment and Discrimination   89
3.3 Unconscious Bias and Microaggressions   92
3.4 Hiring Practices   100
3.5 Bias in Artificial Intelligence (AI)   105
Quiz   111
Chapter Summary   113

4 Equity — 115

    4.1 Equity vs. Equality   119
    4.2 Types of Equity   122
    4.3 Pay Equity and Compensation   128
    4.4 Organizational Impact of Equity Issues   132
    Quiz   134
    Chapter Summary   136

5 Inclusion — 139

    5.1 Intentional Inclusion   142
    5.2 Stereotypes and Stigmas   146
    5.3 Allies, Advocacy, and Anti-Discriminatory Acts   151
    Quiz   155
    Chapter Summary   157

6 Enhanced Diversity Literacy — 159

    6.1 Race   160
    6.2 Age   163
    6.3 Religion   164
    6.4 Gender   165
    6.5 Disabilities and ADA   172
    Quiz   176
    Chapter Summary   179

7 Leveraging Talent — 181

    7.1 Assessment Tools   184
    7.2 Flow   190
    7.3 Cultivate Emotional Intelligence   193
    7.4 Top Performers   194
    7.5 Nontraditional Talent Pools   196
    Quiz   198
    Chapter Summary   201

8 Laws, Practices, and Compliance — 203
- 8.1 Legal Compliance 205
- 8.2 Laws vs. Practices 206
- 8.3 Employer's DE&I Responsibilities 213
- Quiz 215
- Chapter Summary 217

9 Cultural Awareness — 219
- 9.1 Improving Cultural Awareness 223
- 9.2 Community Relations and Impact on the Workplace 226
- Quiz 234
- Chapter Summary 237

10 Systemic Change — 239
- 10.1 Turning the Dial in the Workplace 241
- 10.2 Critical Conversations 244
- 10.3 Training and Development 247
- Quiz 250
- Chapter Summary 253

References — 255
- Books 255
- Magazines 256
- Websites 257

This page is intentionally left blank

Introduction

Although the focus of this book is on diversity in the workplace, diversity is prominent, significant, and encountered in many other environments. It is an aspect of an individual's daily personal life that is taken to work with them consistently.

Some individuals infer a positive correlation between an organization's success and the diversity it embraces. For others, merely hearing the word diversity feels like an imposed buzzword that makes people antsy about getting along at work.

Many organizations and leaders have determined that diversity is essential to a company's growth and overall health. Entities have begun listening to the outpouring cries of their employees and the communities in which they serve and operate. Leaders understand that their role in supporting the organization's evolution requires an authentic desire to promote effective change within and around the company. Additional training, recruitment strategies, and retention efforts are a few ways many organizations address the needs of employees and the community while also leading change. All of these efforts are a response to the realization that embracing and incorporating diversity provides significant benefits to any organization.

Even with so many individuals urging companies to become a more accurate reflection of the diversity that exists in society, there are still many employees and others who have grown weary of the conversations and attention companies are devoting to diversity. To many, talks about diversity may feel like a trendy notion ignited by a workplace buzzword. This book will demonstrate that diversity is much more than a buzzword. In fact, diversity is far too ingrained in historical experiences and cultural identity to marginalize it into a trendy notion of how to improve the work environment. Diversity has been a driving force in workplace decision-making for centuries and remains relevant to the current matters affecting workplace success.

It is no secret that the world is constantly changing. Over the past several decades, organizations have experienced progressive transitions in pay equity laws, women's rights, civil rights, and, more recently, opinions surrounding health and medical independence. The COVID-19 pandemic seemed to disrupt work-life balance when employees had to decide whether to wear a mask at work or risk losing their jobs. Workers faced decisions about taking vaccines to promote safety, choosing remote employment, and childcare alternatives. Many aspects of how people live gradually penetrate the realm of *how they work*, all leading to changes sparking worldwide conversations. Correspondingly, throughout all of the change, diversity lingers in the background, influencing decision after decision in both work and daily living.

To successfully navigate gradual changes and their impact on the workplace, organizations must recognize fluctuations in societal norms, rules, laws, opinions, and individuals' behavior. Failure to detect when changes are occurring otherwise causes companies to suffer stagnated growth and declines in the economic and cultural stability. Therefore, companies must pay closer attention to the positive and negative effects that changes in the environment and society impose on working conditions.

Often, activities occurring in different cultural, economic, political, and social climates manifest through the behaviors and beliefs of individuals. It is difficult to acknowledge and address the workplace impact of climate changes without also understanding how diversity manifests in a person's day-to-day living conditions, holistically.

Progressive companies with visionary leaders can transition and grow to adapt to changes around them. A viable goal for leading organizations is to recognize, respond to, and nurture diversity within individuals that influence the workplace. At work, such diversity among people impacts the ability to create, manage, and grow successful organizations.

Human Resource professionals, managers, and organization leaders all have vested interests in diversity and its impact on a company. However, anyone exploring cultural, social, economic, or political studies will enhance their insights by broadening their diversity literacy.

Diversity in the Workplace introduces easy-to-interpret content that explains critical concepts surrounding identity, diversity, microaggressions, privilege, ethics, inclusion, advocacy, leadership, cultural awareness, corporate responsibility, and other factors that branch from one's individuality. Once people can identify and understand how these aspects of diversity collectively affect a culture, they can be applied to the workplace for improved results.

This page is intentionally left blank

Who can benefit from the book?

This book concisely explains challenging concepts and provides clear examples, so any professional new to the workforce can become aware of and understand diversity literacy. It is also comprehensive enough to offer organizations, leaders, and tenured professionals, deeper insight into the impact of diversity in the workplace that may have traditionally been overlooked, disregarded, or misunderstood.

The book's target audience includes:

- HR Professionals

- Undergraduate and Graduate students focusing on: Business, HR, Ethics, Political Climate, Sociology, Critical Race Theory (CRT), Organizational Development, Organizational Change, Change Management, History (Business Related), or similar disciplines

- Professionals new to the workforce (or recent graduates)

This page is intentionally left blank

How to use the book

This book introduces the historical impact of identity and diversity on the workplace. It provides a firm foundation for individuals and organizations to learn why diversity, equity, and inclusion (DE&I) are essential in the work environment.

- Each chapter progressively explores the importance of understanding how identity and diversity affect individuals at work.

- Readers should read with the intent to enhance knowledge and understanding concerning various types of diversity like race, gender, sexual orientation, age, etc., rather than to determine right vs. wrong.

- Several chapters include a section titled "Reflection" that may focus on the entire chapter or subsections of the chapter. The Reflections section is designed to evoke critical thinking so that readers can demonstrate practical knowledge based on the content from the section.

- Reflection sections do not include answers. However, professors, facilitators, and others may encourage readers to utilize the section for critical thinking exercises and working through scenarios that could present various options.

- In sections concerning workplace decisions, where a scenario is presented and the reader is asked to reflect on options, the reader should take the perspective of an organizational leader, manager, HR professional, or a similar role to determine potential actions based on the scenario. (**Note:** Readers can also reflect on the scenario from an individual perspective, determining possible actions that could be taken if the situation were personal and the reader is now equipped with additional knowledge concerning expectations in the workplace.)

- The book's content does not represent the author's personal, political, social, or other views. It is a compilation of information to enhance the knowledge and understanding of professionals in the workplace concerning diversity, equity, and inclusion.

Chapter 1

Identity

Chapter one introduces the term identity and its significance in understanding diversity. Personal and cultural identity are defined and explained in order to build a foundation for how individuals and groups are perceived within individual communities, society, and the workplace. The content includes historical background, theories, ideas of various academics, and events that have influenced the evolving definition of identity. The chapter outlines key concepts including privilege, white fragility, intersectionality, and multiculturalism, to expound on the perception of identity by oneself and others.

Key learning objectives should include the reader's understanding of the following:

- Definition of key terms: identity, privilege, white fragility, intersectionality, and multiculturalism
- Historical background and significance of individual and cultural identity

- Theories associated with identity formation
- Ways to categorize identity
- Early impact of identity on work and workers
- Different types of privilege commonly associated with the work environment

A logical approach to explaining diversity and its workplace impact begins with understanding identity. It may seem trivial to ask *Who am I?* or *What am I?*, but these questions are foundational for enlightenment concerning oneself and others. Identity is a key component of diversity. In its simplest terms, **identity is defined as the characteristics that describe who someone or what something is.** It includes elements that are inherent to identity such as one's race or eye color. However, a more comprehensive description may expound the definition by adding terms like memories, values, experiences, relationships, beliefs, or awareness to replace or enhance the word characteristics.

Relationships that are cultivated at different stages in life or with different people also make up identity. Assigning titles like parent, co-worker, friend, partner, or supervisor can be how someone may begin to identify their own role in a relationship. Each role is further characterized by expectations ingrained into one's perceived identity.

Specific beliefs, values, or memories may collectively form a version of someone that helps describe their identity. These internal characteristics influence the choices that a person makes throughout their life. However, it is important to note that these descriptors, just like external ones, evolve over time.

Features like height and eye color are also commonly used to describe a person. On most state driver's licenses, government agencies add these external characteristics along with a photographic image to serve as the basis of one's visible identity.

Even with such a broadened scope of descriptors, the definition of identity may still feel somewhat incomplete if a person is asked, "Who are you?" That is because identity could essentially be anything for anyone.

At work, a lack of understanding one's own identity or the critical aspects of others' identity can detrimentally affect an entire organization. It is not essential to know or understand every element of a person that defines them. It is, indeed, impossible. However, learning the aspects of a person's identity that are incorporated into their daily work-life and that help define their role as an employee, co-worker, supervisor, boss, or customer is pertinent for evaluating diversity in the workplace.

The Iceberg Example

A common reference that helps unveil the mystery of identity is the iceberg. An iceberg is a large piece of ice that sits in the middle of a larger body of water. The small portion of the frozen-solid mass visible above the waterline is referred to as the tip of the iceberg. The tip is typically only one-eighth of the entire iceberg, so the majority of the mass floats below the water's surface. The hidden portion may take many shapes and can be extremely dangerous to travelers if they make wrong assumptions regarding its size or strength.

Figure 1.1

The tip of the iceberg presents an outward visible descriptor.

The layer that floats beneath the water makes up the majority of the iceberg and is not outwardly visible, yet is massive and comprises various other descriptors.

Ship meets an iceberg - infographic template By lenoleum – Adobe Stock File #:162757715

Similar to the iceberg example, individuals have features that appear evident to others. However, those external features make up only a small portion of the person's identity. The unseen characteristics like values, beliefs, and experiences account for just as much in ascertaining a person's true identity.

Categorizing Identity

What makes sense? How can I figure it all out? These questions speak to the natural human inclination to find meaning in the things around them. Seeking connections and correlations is how many people rationalize the world. Even infants, who may not know the definitions or use for specific objects, have a natural inclination. If they are hungry, a toddler may put things into their mouth. Sometimes they even do it when they are not hungry. However, something motivated them to figure out if the object in front of them and their ability to place the object in their mouth would work well together. The unexplainable desire to form a connection between two or more things is how we begin to categorize those things.

First, determining that things with different characteristics can be separated from things that have similar characteristics allows those things to be sorted. Sorting requires identifying and comparing features that are distinctly different from one thing and the next so that each distinctive feature can be categorized.

There are countless ways to categorize identity. A witness to a hit and run accident may describe a vehicle as red or blue. The vehicle may be a car or a truck, or large or small - all these descriptors are seemingly straightforward. However, when talking about a person, the same witness may refer to a driver as the victim or perpetrator. They may describe characteristics traditionally associated with a male or female, such as a beard or color of make-up. Although these descriptors may also seem, at first glance, straightforward, they could be far more complex depending on a myriad of factors.

Referring to previous examples, the ways in which identity could be sorted are based on a person's visible characteristics and those that are not visible. Although these two categories may seem relatively simple, categorizing them is more complex. Just like in the iceberg example, it would be a mistake not to consider various aspects of what is unseen.

For now, think of identity using three very large buckets: 1) things that are visible, seen, or observed 2) things that are not visible or able to be seen or observed, and 3) what is believed, perceived, or assumed. You can begin to sort almost anything using these three broad categories. Still, it gets tricky, because as you will learn later, every aspect of identity is not always evident enough to categorize.

A More Heroic Example of Identity

Use Clark Kent, for example. If you have no idea who he is, then discussing identity is perfect because you get to figure it out. If you are familiar with his character, this example should help broaden your knowledge about identity.

On the surface, Clark Kent is a man traditionally defined by his shy, modest, and common behavior. He wears glasses, stumbles, and has a regular job as a reporter. He is often described as handsome and mild-mannered. Clark Kent grew up on a farm and was adopted by two loving parents who happened to stumble across him after he was abandoned on their farmland as an infant.

Each of these descriptive characteristics can be categorized and put into the bucket for things seen or observed. They include Clark's mannerisms, physical attributes, relationship roles, and other identifiers that others can visually or interpersonally interpret.

Relying only on the bucket that holds visible or observed interpretations of one's identity leads to a failure in understanding and acknowledging true identity. For instance, Clark also has an alter ego, Superman. While Clark and Superman are indeed one in the same person, not all of the traits that give Clark his superhuman abilities are visible. Imagine that Clark Kent never had a red cape, tights, or took off his glasses. Would that stop him from possessing the characteristics that most people associate with Superman? For instance, Clark has superhuman strength, heat and x-ray vision, super hearing, and even the ability to fly. Without ever witnessing Clark Kent do any of these things, would he still possess all of these abilities and characteristics? The answer is yes. Dressed and operating under the visible guise of Clark Kent, he would still possess all of the internal (unseen) characteristics and abilities of Superman.

Figure 1.2

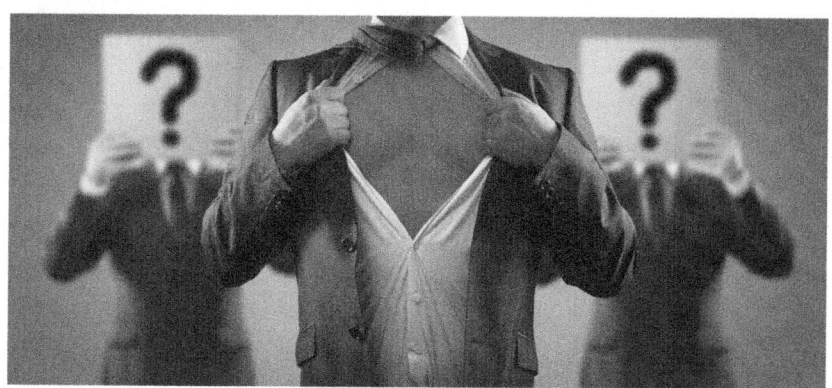

Who is super businessman By chones – Adobe Stock File #: 51248912

There are now two buckets of identifiers. Those that can visibly be seen or interpreted and those that Clark Kent still possesses but that are not visible or immediately observed. Clark's alter ego abilities and characteristics as Superman can go in the bucket of things unseen.

Finally, the third bucket holds beliefs, perceptions, and assumptions. Start with Clark's beliefs. Even if he is not dressed up in his cape, does Clark believe he can fly? Does he believe he can hold a busload of kids in the air? What about the people who have heard stories about someone who flies through the air but have never witnessed it for themselves? Do they believe Clark Kent could have these capabilities? Could some people assume that because he can fly and lift a bus that he is also completely invincible?

Clark's beliefs about himself, perceptions that others gather from stories they have heard, or even the assumptions that people make are all important, because they do not have to be seen to become defining descriptors for Clark's identity. They are still elements of what makes Clark Kent who he is. They are still elements of what makes Clark Kent and others believe Clark can do what he can do.

Identity At Work

Perhaps for Clark Kent, it was rough growing up having to hide all of his experiences and hidden talents. Although he made a conscious effort to hide them for his safety, privacy, or other reasons, hiding them did not negate them. In the workplace, there are millions of Clark Kents. Not all of them have superhuman abilities, and in most cases, you will never see coworkers or team members put on a red cape. However, some people do have exceptional talents, characteristics, and skills. Some people may deliberately shelter aspects of their identity while others may want to express elements of what makes them unique.

Talents come in the form of specialized knowledge, skills, and abilities. For example, describing someone with good listening and communication skills could be the defining descriptor differentiating between a good therapist and one who is not as skilled at their job. All of the characteristics that uniquely define who or what a person is helps to identify them. Identity is, therefore, something that is broadened in scope by both the possessor of the characteristics and the interpreter distinguishing the characteristics.

At work, identity is also expressed in many forms, which we will discuss throughout this book. Learning more about identity will provide a solid foundation for understanding diversity. Employers categorize individuals before they are even a part of a company. They start with the recruitment process. Sometimes individuals are categorized by educational credentials, such as those having a degree or certification. For certain companies, there are efforts to hire veterans, disabled or bilingual individuals. These distinguishing factors are all elements of identity, and subsequently, diversity, among applicants, candidates, or employees. As we move forward, you will learn how identity and diversity have historically impacted organizations. Professionals seeking to understand diversity better must be open to learning about various aspects of personal identity that make each person uniquely diverse.

1.1 Historical Background of Identity and Diversity

How Identity Is Formed

Now that you know that identity can be made up of many things, it is equally important to understand how identity is formed. Some aspects of identity are assigned at birth (or soon after), such as a person's name. Also, at birth, doctors will typically assign a sex, such as male or female, which can be a descriptive identifier for a long time. However, even one's assigned sex does not confirm their complete identity.

Personal identity or self-identity is also influenced by parents, peers, childhood experiences, experimentation in adolescence, and many other factors. Scholars have shared several theories about how identity is formed and based their lifelong work on understanding its effects on individuals.

Sigmund Freud (1856-1939) is the founding father of psychoanalysis, which is, among other things, a theory that explains human behavior. According to Freud's psychoanalytic framework, the human mind is made up of three parts, the id, ego, and superego. Freud proposed that each part is driven by different motives.

1. The Id is driven by instinct and desire
2. The Superego is driven by morality and values, and
3. The Ego moderates both the id and superego and creates one's identity

Freud further contended that events in a person's childhood greatly influence their adult life and help shape their personality.

Figure 1.3

Id - Ego - Superego

- **Id:** Instinctive from birth, primitive, primal desires, seeks pleasure-avoids pain
  - "Unconscious"

- **Ego:** Awareness of one's self and ability to interact with the world, driven by the 'reality principle', exists in both the conscience and unconscious
  - "Balance id and superego"

- **Superego:** Internalization of the moral rules of society, last part of personality to develop, concerned with morality, right and wrong
  - "Conscience"

Like Freud, others have explored theories about identity and its formation. Psychologist, Erik Erikson (1902 – 1994), proposed a development theory based on different stages of life. He coined the term **ego identity**, a conscious sense of the merged different versions of oneself that are developed through social interaction and that constantly change due to new experiences and information acquired in daily interactions with others.

Erikson divided the lifecycle into eight stages that each contained a conflict. According to his psychosocial theory, at each stage of the lifecycle, individuals experience and need to resolve a different type of conflict. To progress through the life cycle successfully, individuals would need to apply a resolution. Successfully resolving the conflict added to the healthy development of their personality and a sense of competence. Erikson believed that the main conflict that occurs during adolescence is identity versus role confusion and failure to master the conflicts at the adolescent stage would lead to feelings of inadequacy.

Adolescents have long faced challenges with forming identity. Insurmountable obstacles and conflicts arise during the adolescent phase which often is a roadblock to fully conquering the many aspects that form one's identity. Social media, schools, family structures, religious institutions, and even employers contribute to forming adolescent identity. Making decisions such as which sports to play, which friend groups to establish, or what religious affiliation one would like to have, are all conflicts that may present themselves to adolescents. In many cases, by the time some of these conflicts are resolved, an adolescent has begun to transition into adulthood. At that point, there are new and equally challenging conflicts to conquer.

In adulthood, individuals may struggle with career choices, the decision to become a parent, retirement, socio-economic responsibilities, and more. Based on Erikson's and Freud's theories about identity and the many aspects that it can encompass, it is clear that identity is formed in different ways. It is essential to understand that identity is not an immediate creation but is developmental in nature, as, over time, it builds on changing appearances, experiences, and beliefs. Identity is therefore formed at various stages by exploring different options and committing to an option based upon the outcome of the exploration. This exploration does not consider specific identifying characteristics such as those assigned at birth by another individual.

Early Impact of Identity on Work

Throughout history, race, skin color, language, ethnicity, and other outward-facing characteristics have long been sources for identifying and categorizing workers. The early 1600s are widely regarded as a landmark, representing what has become acknowledged as the beginning of slavery in America. Although there are several accounts of other acts of slavery before the 1600s, 1619 is documented as a timeframe when human cargo of enslaved persons was brought to colonies to perform work functions for other individuals or entities.

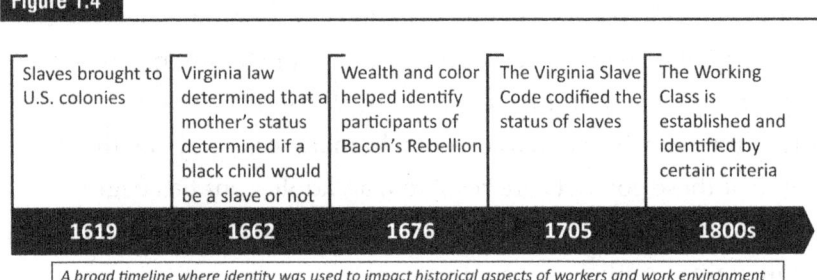

Figure 1.4

Slaves brought to U.S. colonies	Virginia law determined that a mother's status determined if a black child would be a slave or not	Wealth and color helped identify participants of Bacon's Rebellion	The Virginia Slave Code codified the status of slaves	The Working Class is established and identified by certain criteria
1619	1662	1676	1705	1800s

A broad timeline where identity was used to impact historical aspects of workers and work environment

The most prominent distinguishing characteristic that determined who was enslaved versus who was not was skin color or race. Africans, now referred to by some as African Americans or Black people, were identified by their skin color, origin, and other factors such as the language they spoke. Among other identifying characteristics, these prominent descriptors made it relatively simple to distinguish the expectation for who would work, the types of work they would do, and to establish a sense of either inferiority or superiority.

In 1662, a Virginia law relied on the specific identity associated with race and status to dictate that the mother's status determined if a Black child would be enslaved. Later, in 1676, individuals whose identity was tied to wealth and color were used to identify participants of Bacon's Rebellion in Virginia. Poor whites and Black people fought together, prompting the government's response to expedite the transition to Black slavery.

In 1705, The Virginia Slave Code codified the status of slaves, further limited their freedom, and included provisions stating that non-Christians brought to Virginia would be slaves. In this instance, one's religious affiliation or identity as a Christian was used to determine enslavement.

These examples indicate how a person's identity, whether self-proclaimed or perceived by others, resulted in the enslavement and use of humans as a workforce. In these early years, slavery was a major labor source for farming. Slave owners or individuals in charge of overseeing the labor force were not seemingly concerned with slave workers' wellness, health, pay, self-worth, working hours, or any other aspect that would promote a sense of value and belonging for the slaves. Slaves were stripped of familial ties, clothing, safety, and in just about every case, their names. This process of stripping identity was an effort to create and establish new ones that would be governed by someone else's perception of who and what a slave would be.

Figure 1.5

Slavery - Esclaves - Sklaven - 19th century By Erica Guilane-Nachez – Adobe Stock File #: 60745132

A person's identity as a slave, African, Black person, woman, or child could quickly compel them to feel inferior, especially in cases where these identifiers were the fuel for mistreatment, abuse, and other punishments. To avoid various punishments, slaves could choose to embrace their perceived identity and work relentlessly to please slave masters. Some, however, chose to embrace their identity as defined prior to being enslaved and rebelled, revolted or ran away. The slaves that chose the latter likely did so because their self-identity in its fullness did not align with the imposed or perceived identity as determined by slave owners. The desire to be seen and treated differently was a direct result of the slaves' self-proclaimed identity and worth. However, for a long time, African slaves concealed many other aspects of their identity that had previously been hidden for self-preservation and protection. The hope of creating a more tolerant society within the United States and the Americas that could slowly embrace parts of them became a goal as slaves continued to form, reestablish and reclaim their identity.

Creating the Working Class

According to Karl Marx (1818–1883), the working class was the foundation of society's wealth. Their textile goods, labor-power, skills, and services resulted in the emergence of a class of laborers who began to form communities of like-minded individuals.

In the early 20th century, the working class responded to rapidly changing political, economic, and social climates. The instinct was to protect what they had worked for and to build identities and cultures that would address the challenges they faced.

The communities and groups that the workers formed included diversity in terms of gender, race, ethnicity, and class. The groups and individuals within them were affected by the approaching industrial era, which included conflicts over immigration, the place of former slaves in a changing society, technological advancements, political influences, and other swiftly changing norms.

Although different identities within the groups highlighted the ways in which individuals were different, the diversity among the groups continued to grow to meet a common goal. The commonality was that the individuals within the groups were members of a collective class of laborers who would forge their way in life.

By 1900 to 1945, the working class in the United States had formed its own identity by pushing to attain political, economic, and cultural influence. Their collective identity was established to solidify their position in society.

1.2 Privilege and White Fragility

Privilege is a primarily unearned right, immunity, benefit, or advantage enjoyed by a particular person, class, or a restricted group of people over another person or group that is not afforded the same right, immunity, benefit or advantage. Understanding the importance of privilege and its effects in the workplace will help learners form a correlation between identity, diversity, and workplace impact. Although privilege can span a myriad of forms and examples, there are specific types of privilege that directly impact the work environment, including:

- **White privilege** - A type of privilege benefiting white people at the expense of other races, that is not afforded to other races without some form of disadvantage or repercussion to the other race (ex: a white person yelling offensively at a law enforcement officer and threatening to have the officer fired, with no repercussion from the officer)

- **Religious privilege** - A type of privilege afforded to individuals whose religion or religious affiliation is valued over others, or that is assumed to be the societal "norm" where other religions are not valued or treated the same (ex: recognizing Christmas as an official company holiday, while not recognizing other religious holidays or treating employees who observe them with equal entitlement)

- **Gender privilege** - A type of privilege usually referring to benefits or advantages distributed to or experienced by men based on their gender

- **Heterosexual privilege** - A type of privilege describing the advantages favorably granted to someone because of their heterosexual orientation

- **Socio-economic privilege** - A type of privilege referring to predictors for wealth attainment, such as income, status, family background, occupation, education, and other factors

In society, almost everyone has some level of privilege. It may be tied to the area in which a person grew up as a child, the schools they attended, the family they were born into, or even opportunities they were afforded in life. These different privileges may often go unnoticed by those individuals receiving them until someone from a class or group who does not have the same privilege expresses concern. It is crucial that individuals who have certain privileges are aware of them but not misinformed about what the privilege means or society's perception about it.

Often, conversations about diversity are likened to a two-sided coin where one group or individual feels targeted and ridiculed, while the other individual or group feels unheard, discriminated against or disregarded. Typically, the group that feels unheard, discriminated against or disregarded is the marginalized group or marginalized population. A **marginalized group** experiences discrimination and social, political and economic exclusion because of unequal power relationships across economic, political, social, racial and cultural dimensions. Painful conversations emerge from both perspectives as each attempts to justify and explain their position.

At work, avoiding the conversation or failing to acknowledge privileges will only fuel misconception on one side that they do not exist or are not important, and on the other side that a group or individual is not worthy of being heard. Companies and their leaders must encourage their teams to understand such elements of diversity and manage them accordingly.

What comes to mind when you think about executives? Do CEOs, CFOs, and other executives have any privileges? What about the men at work when compared to the women? Have you ever noticed that people with certain religious beliefs feel more connected to the company?

These types of questions are not unfamiliar. They remain in the minds of individuals who do not get to partake in the advantages clearly afforded to others. As a leader in an organization, it is difficult to manage the effects that these facts or perceptions may have in the workplace, if you do not first understand your own privilege. Your unique experience and connection to privilege help craft the experience of your workplace peers.

It is equally important to note that privilege does not inherently mean that an individual or group has received something physically or materially. Individuals may have privileges that are less evident to some, yet obvious to others. For example, seeing racial or gender representation of one's self in a meeting, on a print ad, or in a television commercial is a privilege that is not afforded to every person or group. Society's representation of the norm surrounds individuals in their day-to-day living. When the norm is not representative of one's self, an individual may realize that they lack a certain privilege. Likewise, it is important for individuals with certain privileges to realize they exist, even if they are not inherently apparent to the individuals who possess them.

Recognizing Privilege

Employees at all levels in an organization should be inclined to ask themselves, "Do I have a level of privilege?" Doing so not only shows a valiant effort to join the conversation about diversity and inclusion but also leans toward personal enlightenment about one's place and value in the conversation.

The easiest way to approach the question is to first determine if, as an individual or part of a group, you have certain rights, advantages, benefits, or exemptions that are not afforded to someone in a different group. A common misperception of determining privilege is that the individual who has it either asked for it, sought it, or fought for it. In many cases, it is the opposite, leaving the privileged person or groups to defend their lack of involvement in obtaining such privilege. For example, white privilege is a prevalent construct in both society and the work environment. While it is evident to some, it is seemingly nonexistent to others. To determine if it truly exists and if a person is entitled to such privilege, they should merely determine if being white (or the perception of such identity) allows for advantages over individuals who are not identified in the same manner.

In the workplace, white privilege is often associated with hiring decisions, promotion determinations, perceived skills and competency, and industry acceptance. Individuals who are not white may find it more difficult to prove themselves in the medical field as a doctor or the legal field as an attorney when compared to their white counterparts. Individuals of color may find that they did not receive promotions or job offers compared to applicants with similar or lesser skills and credentials.

In society, examples such as being presumed to be guilty or suspicious-looking when shopping at a store or casually walking in a crowd of people are commonly prevalent. Persons of color have often been targeted, while white individuals are less likely to be presumed as guilty of acting or looking suspicious. Lack of white privilege can therefore cause individuals to feel and act defensively to prove that the privilege is unfair and exists.

Other forms of privilege are also rooted in the advantages that individuals have over others. Gender privilege has traditionally been tied to men having certain advantages that women do not. Issues in pay equity, perceptions about competence, role assignment, and group membership are primary areas where women, femmes, or non-men have been denied advancement due to male privilege.

Have you ever wondered why certain companies recognize holidays like Christmas or Thanksgiving, but not Kwanza, Hanukkah, or Ramadan and Eid al-Fitr? It is likely because the organization was founded by individuals who are not religiously devoted to recognizing or honoring the other holidays. It is possible that the organization leaders are not aware or vested in the holidays enough to make them universally celebratory as they may be for individuals with specific religions. Religious privilege includes feeling a sense of connection between your religious celebrations and broader society. For example, automatically having a day off from work for one group's observed religious holiday is a religious privilege. Although other individuals may share in the day off, if the holiday is not tied to their particular religion, they are experiencing the result of the religious privilege of another group.

Socio-economic privilege is a little different for everyone. On the surface, it would appear that anyone with the financial means to buy, do, or go where they want because of their ability to pay for it, has a socio-economic advantage or privilege.

Consider a private school that receives adequate funding compared to a public school that does not. A school that does not receive sufficient funding may be considered low-performing because it does not have certain resources that aid in increasing performance. An example would be an inventory of computers or books that students need to complete tasks or to enhance learning. The school that has such resources also has students who have a socioeconomic privilege. Although students may be unaware of such privilege, it exists, and is often evident to students in lower-performing schools who lack funding and resources.

All privilege is not specific to one particular group. However, in the workplace, again, certain privileges are much more prevalent and worthy of deep, constructive conversation to move the needle toward positive change.

To recognize your privilege, you should determine all of the things that privilege is not. It is not a deliberate attempt to belittle someone. It is not an assumption that the privileged individual sought out the privilege. Privilege is not strictly related to heirship or economic stability. Privilege is not an admission of guilt or wrong-doing. It is also not an indicator that individuals have not been subjected to challenges, struggles or injustices in their own experiences.

A privileged individual can still recognize, become aware, and manage their privilege without dismissing its existence. Acknowledging when privilege exists can help increase self-awareness and the awareness of perspectives that are different from one's own. According to Lee Jourdan, in an article about diversity and inclusion titled, "Talk About Privilege at Work," acknowledging privilege can also help lower defenses, demonstrate vulnerability, and set the tone for inclusive behaviors.

To determine your privilege, you should consider aspects of your identity, including race, gender, sexuality, physical ability, socioeconomic status, education level, and other factors that are a distinct advantage over others. Recognizing and acknowledging your privileges relative to others leaves the door open to recognizing the advantages and opportunities that coworkers, team members, and others may be restricted from.

White Fragility

In 2011, Dr. Robin DiAngelo, a US academic and educator, coined the term white fragility. It is defined as the discomfort and defensiveness of a white person when confronted with information about racial inequality and injustice.

White fragility significantly relates to identity, diversity, and privilege. Acknowledging and discussing the impact of white fragility is critical in conversations about racial equality, racism, historical impact, and privilege. Dr. DiAngelo further contends that white fragility promotes racism. Her initial assessment has become a shared belief among various marginalized groups who continue to experience racism, sometimes at the hands of white fragility.

Addressing this notion attempts to pull the veil from what has traditionally been offensive to individuals of other races or ethnicities. According to Jessica Caporuscio, an internal medicine specialist and clinical pharmacist with a doctorate in pharmacy, "White people in the United States have protection from racial stress." However, to build on the progressive efforts to correct historical injustices, present-day lack of awareness, empathy, or understanding, it is crucial to identify, explore and overcome white fragility.

Sentiments about diversity and inclusion regarding the workplace stem from societal behaviors that are an outward expression of how individuals and groups feel about diversity and inclusion in general. Therefore, the effort to address issues in the workplace requires deeper conversations that do not shy away from the truths about identity, privilege, white fragility, and their impact.

It is important to note that although they are related, white fragility is not the same as racism. It is also not the same as white privilege, white superiority, or white supremacy. Instead, white **fragility** is a state in which white people respond to triggers associated with their own identity. As discussed before, white privilege refers to the benefits, advantages, or exemptions white people have in society that are not afforded to other people of different races. White supremacy is a perception or belief that people with white skin are superior to others.

Thinking back to earlier sections of this book, you discovered that identity is formed in many different ways and at different stages in life. Consider a white man raised on a farm near an all-white community who had never met an Asian, Black, or Indian person. Simply not having met or been around other races or ethnicities does not make the white individual a racist. Nor does it keep the individual from forming an identity throughout his life. However, a lack of education, informed perspectives, experiences, or awareness about racial injustices, racism, inequalities and other prevalent cultural matters will undoubtedly leave the man lacking knowledge essential in preparing him for other encounters.

Imagine that one day, after the young man reaches age 20, he is offered a job that requires him to travel away from the farm to a big city, like New York. New York is an extremely diverse city. Individuals of various races, genders, religious affiliations, and backgrounds make up a large numerical majority of the population. Imagine if within his first day in the new city, he encounters a person of a different race who says to him that a comment he made was evidence of his white privilege or that the only reason the young man got his new job is because he is white. How do you think the young man would feel?

In this case, the white man may feel saddened, upset, angry, defensive, or any number of other emotions. That is because his experience may or may not be the same as the perception of the individual of color. The white man may believe that his comments were socially or culturally acceptable. He may be certain that his background, experience, and education was the reason for solidifying the new job. However, it is important to know that although having different emotions about a situation is acceptable, those feelings do not excuse or make the comments he may have said acceptable. The goal of addressing white fragility is both to bring forth an awareness and refrain from or stop coddling the defensive emotional reaction of white people to such awareness.

When individuals of different races engage in conversations about racial injustices, racism, inequality, or other socially-charged topics, they may trigger many responses. The concept of white fragility presumes that when these types of conversations are held with white individuals or if a white person is the subject of the conversation, it may cause the individual to become uncomfortable, triggering defensive actions. Other emotions may also surface, such as shame, fear, regret, anger, rage, sadness, or even silence. Even when such emotional reactions occur, conversations are still necessary to address various topics. Discussions should not stop because of white fragility, but instead be enhanced.

The difficulty with having critical conversations that open the lines of communication about racial injustices lies in the responses that individuals or groups with opposing perspectives may have. If a person of color makes a statement that triggers an angered or defensive response from a white person, then the conversation may not be constructive or productive. Similarly, if a white person avoids conversation or responds in an off-putting manner about socially-charged topics, it may feel to a person of color that the white person is again exercising a privilege that shelters them from what others have had to endure for a long time.

Racial stressors that cause reactions by white persons may prevent people of color from attempting to talk about racism with them altogether. This result is, therefore, a barrier to progressive strides in communication, racial equality, valuing diversity, and other societal, social, and cultural goals.

According to an article by Jessica Caporuscio, white people can experience stressors or triggers from:

- a person claiming that a white person's views are racist
- a person of color talking about their racial experiences and perspectives
- a person of color not protecting a white person's feelings about racism
- a fellow white person not agreeing with another white person's perspectives on racism
- a white person receiving feedback that their behavior or actions had a racist impact
- situations where a person of color is driving the story's action or is in a non-stereotypical role

Historically, white people have not endured the same level or types of discrimination or oppression for similar lengths of time that other races have experienced. White privilege long sheltered the groups from societal and cultural experiences that many others were exposed to and subsequently built up a tolerance against. The tolerance also included a heightened understanding of how privilege looked and felt.

The different triggers and stressors that white people experience as a part of white fragility result from not having to endure similar inequalities and conversations that other races have encountered. White people were therefore not equipped to hear instances where their race would not be revered as powerful or supreme. Thus, the actions, conversations and triggers cause white people to be fragile in their ability to accept, understand, or even listen to individuals who challenge their perception of their identity. A white person's lack of experiencing racism directly often causes them to overlook it, not understand it, or deny its existence.

Whereas a white person may not be racist, experiencing white fragility can contribute to racism. Actions such as becoming defensive, avoiding a topic, denying white privilege, or claiming to be the victim of a racially charged conversation can all contribute to racism, perpetuating the very element that presents a barrier to progress.

Many stressors and triggers cause white fragility. It is not often intentional on the part of persons exhibiting it. However, failure to recognize it and how to manage it is detrimental. If the objective is to create a more diverse, inclusive, and embracing culture, white fragility must be recognized and addressed. The goal is then to become aware of white privilege and to identify, explore and overcome white fragility. It is crucial for white persons not to avoid uncomfortable conversations and to understand that when they arise, the attempts by other races to engage in the conversation are most often to enforce progress, not punishment.

1.3 Intersectionality

When discussing identity, privilege, and diversity, several other concepts are relevant to fully grasp how to embrace and incorporate diversity into daily living and workplace environments. At work, the most common awareness for many is related to race, gender, and sexual orientation—however, there are many other forms of diversity and subsequently, oppression that exist.

Intersectionality is a term that was coined by Professor Kimberle Crenshaw in 1989. It was subsequently added to the Oxford Dictionary in 2015. Intersectionality is a concept that the different types of oppression placed on individuals are all linked. Oxford defines **intersectionality** as "the interconnected nature of social categorizations such as race, class, and gender, regarded as creating overlapping and interdependent systems of discrimination or disadvantage."

In the previous section, we learned about white privilege and white fragility. The focus on race may have inferred that most oppression is emitted from white individuals, whereas other races are the target of that oppression. This section exposes an even larger notion that oppression is not one-sided. Racism does not exist with only one race dishing out the behavioral atrocities. Additionally, other forms of discrimination are not all issued by a single group or person. They are, however, spread among any person or group who does not share the common identifying characteristics as the targeted person or group.

Intersectionality acknowledges that everyone has their own unique set of experiences tied to discrimination and oppression of their identity. If elements of that identity are also associated with a marginalized group, such as race, gender, class, sexual orientation, or physical ability, then discrimination or oppression can be imposed from many perspectives.

Intersectionality addresses the conceptual identity of a person or group that is affected by multiple forms of discrimination. Overlapping identity characteristics such as race and sexual orientation or race and gender present an even more profound challenge to understanding diversity.

Think about specific job industries. There are some in which certain genders are much more prevalent than others. In other cases, race, status, class, and physical ability seem to prevail in the industry. Conversations about intersectionality can be ignited by asking a person's perception of what identity characteristics the following are likely to have:

- Professional basketball players
- Truck drivers
- Ballet dancers
- IT or Computer technology professionals
- Doctors
- Opera singers
- Construction workers
- Nurses

Although many people can fit these descriptors, there are differentiators like race, gender, and physical abilities that are typically affiliated with specific jobs or industries. An individual who holds any position could experience multiple forms of oppression or discrimination because various aspects of their identity are opposite of what is traditionally accepted or used to define the role.

An Asian, transgender, female, professional basketball player, who only speaks Mandarin, for example, may encounter:

1. Pay equity issues (lesser pay than male basketball players)

2. Pay equity issues (lesser pay than white female basketball players)

3. Harassing or discriminatory actions against her from team members or co-workers based on her sexual orientation or transgender identity

4. Discriminatory or bias behavior based on the language she speaks (or cannot speak)

Each of these characteristics helps identify the person. However, each identifier is also a way in which intersectionality is demonstrated. All of the distinguishing characteristics are intertwined, yet each serves as a different target for potentially oppressive or discriminatory behaviors. Individuals associate with, identify with, and belong to different groups at the same time.

Figure 1.6

Intersectional Word Cloud on a white background. By arloo – Adobe Stok File #: 424895451

It is, therefore, essential to consider intersectionality when examining the social construct related to workplace equity. It is not enough to only identify and recognize a person's race or gender. It is equally important to know when multiple factors exist that create the potential for an individual to be considered a member of a marginalized group. Failing to realize when intersectionality exists can lead to perpetuated inequities and injustices toward other groups with which a person may be associated.

To support diversity at work, identity, white privilege, white fragility, and intersectionality should all be explored. For example, assumptions that all Asian people feel or believe the same thing is easily refuted by adding intersectionality. A bi-sexual Asian person will likely have additional oppression if they are also, for example, a woman with a disability. Their unique experience brings forth an identity that does not conform to a society only addressing Asian hate or only discussing women's rights.

Conversations about intersectionality should not be about whether or not you agree or disagree with people's intersecting identities, as they should be about understanding the importance of having the conversations.

1.4 Multiculturalism

To build on the concept of intersectionality, multiculturalism offers an additional aspect of one's identity that should be acknowledged when attempting to embrace, value, or understand diversity and its workplace impact. Multiculturalism is key to achieving increased cultural diversity. A society striving for such diversity appreciation also values the cultural differences among groups within the society.

Multiculturalism has multiple meanings in different contexts. In sociology, **multiculturalism** describes how society deals with cultural diversity within a community and at a national level. In political philosophy, multiculturalism refers to how societies formulate and implement official policies dealing with the equitable treatment of different cultures.

Different cultures respond to the same stressors or stimuli with different actions. This is typically because individuals in multicultural communities learn, share, and teach information differently within particular cultures. As information and ways of life are passed down or celebrated, so are traditions, behaviors, and things like artifacts or styles of music.

With such variances among cultures, certain actions may trigger a reaction from a certain culture that is different from an expected or likely reaction from another culture, and the postulation is that different cultures can coexist peacefully to encourage cultural diversity. There is an assumption that society as a whole, benefits from increased diversity through the harmonious coexistence of different cultures.

How Multiculturalism Is Formed

Multiculturalism may occur naturally through immigration or by design when jurisdictions of different cultures are combined through legislative decree. It is typically developed according to one of two theories: 1) The Melting Pot theory or 2) the Salad Bowl theory.

The **Melting Pot theory** suggests that various immigrant groups will tend to "melt together" and abandon their individual cultures to become fully assimilated into the predominant society. The theory has been criticized for suggesting that groups should or will abandon their traditions and other characteristics of their identity to accomplish peaceful integration into society. It diminishes the notion of embracing diversity.

The **Salad Bowl theory** is representative of a heterogeneous society in which people coexist but retain at least some of the unique characteristics of their traditional culture and identity. This theory is more widely appreciated when examining diversity, as it does not require people to individually or collectively let go of their cultural identity to assimilate into the dominant society.

Quiz

1. True or False. It is essential for organizations to understand every aspect of an employee's identity to ensure they are always acting in the employee's best interest.

   a. True

   b. False

2. Carrie is the Marketing Director at her company. She asked her colleagues to serve on an interview panel to help her select and hire a manager that would report directly to her. When Carrie held a brief meeting to discuss the interview process, her expectations, and identifying the perfect candidate, she referenced an iceberg example. Which of the following was most likely Carrie's point concerning the iceberg example?

   a. It is best to hire individuals who have global experience, especially those from different continents

   b. It is important to unveil the unseen characteristics about an individual that may be good or bad for the role.

   c. There are many layers to a job. Employees should not just focus on the main task at hand

   d. Hiring the perfect candidate is a science, similar to the science of how an iceberg is formed

3. Which of the following best represent broad ways to categorize identity?

    a. Things that are Visible, Things that are Not Visible, and Things that are Believed

    b. Things that are Observed and Things that are Not Visible

    c. Things that are Visible, Things that are Imagined, and Things that are Hoped For

    d. Things that are Visible, Things that are Believed, Things that are Discovered

4. Which word is best described as an advantage, benefit, or right that a person or group has over another person or group?

    a. Equality

    b. Intersectionality

    c. Fragility

    d. Marginalization

    e. Privilege

5. **Which statement is False?**

   a. Some males have privilege over females

   b. Some females have privilege over males

   c. Most people have some type of privilege

   d. Most people do not have privilege over others

| Answers | 1 – b | 2 – b | 3 – a | 4 – e | 5 – d |

Detailed Explanation to the above questions can be downloaded from the **Online Resources** *section of this book on* **www.vibrantpublishers.com**

Chapter Summary

- Identity is a key component of diversity.

- Various descriptors make up identity, including physical characteristics, values, beliefs, experiences, religion, background, status, race, ethnicity, gender, and other things that describe a person or group.

- The majority of a person's identity is unseen or not visible.

- Identity can be categorized into three large buckets: 1) Things that are seen, visible, or observed 2) Things not visible or able to be seen or observed, and 3) What is believed, perceived, or assumed.

- Individuals or groups may shelter or hide aspects of their identity for various reasons, including protection or privacy.

- Academics like Sigmund Freud and Erik Erikson have contributed to concepts and theories concerning identity.

- Historically, identity impacted work and the practice of slavery, as slaves and workers were categorized by identifying characteristics such as skin color, national origin, class, or status.

- Understanding and acknowledging one's own privileges is pertinent to addressing privileges, or lack thereof, of others.

- ◆ Critical conversations concerning white fragility, racism, and racially charged topics should occur to move toward diversity and inclusion progress.
- ◆ It is essential to consider intersectionality when examining the social construct related to workplace equity.

This page is intentionally left blank

Chapter 2

Diversity

Chapter two explores the definition of diversity and outlines various examples of diversity typically encountered within the workplace. Each section details the importance of how diversity directly impacts individuals, companies, and the work environment. The chapter incorporates real-world scenarios and examples for reflection.

Key learning objectives should include the reader's understanding of the following:

- Definition of key terms: diversity, physical appearance and attributes, physical and mental abilities, sex and gender, age, race, ethnicity and nationality, status, language and communication, spirituality and religion, socioeconomic background, learning style, working style, talents, skills and attitude, EQ and IQ

- Comparison of sex and gender

- Comparison of race, ethnicity, and nationality

- Different learning styles

- The importance of each example of diversity within the workplace
- How to address challenges and leverage each element of diversity within the workplace

Diversity is everything about the human race that makes one individual or group different from another individual or group. People are diverse in many ways, and there is no perfect indicator to quantify every factor of diversity. When most people hear the word diversity, they may only think about race, gender, age, or sexual orientation. However, diversity can encompass beliefs, physical abilities, religious affiliation, values, national origin, class, gender identity, ethnicity, experiences, and many other elements that up a person or group's identity.

Diversity is prominent throughout society, as individuals display variety in their preferences related to fashion, music, food, entertainment, etc. Think about how people utilize dating apps. The premise is to put in all of the information that makes a person uniquely different from others on the app, yet, hoping to find someone who shares their similar interests or preferences. The app relies on diversity to distinguish potential matches from non-matches and focuses on preferences to make the final connection. Some individuals seek a match with diverse experiences from their own, while others seek matches based on similar experiences and commonalities.

In the workplace, companies behave similarly. When they determine a need for an individual to fill a position, they have to identify all of the unique characteristics that the person should have to fulfill the position and company needs adequately. Sometimes a company seeks out an individual who can speak multiple languages. Other times, they may look for someone who has similar skills or attributes to a person who is in an identical role already. Diversity is what allows companies to make more perfect matches for their needs.

The workplace tends to focus on specific types of diversity, such as educational background, certain competencies or skills, and even physical abilities for specific positions. However, to expand the concept and benefit of diversity, it is critical to broaden the scope of the value diversity brings to an organization. It is essential to learn different aspects of diversity that may have traditionally been overlooked, disregarded, or unknown. Doing so will substantially increase a company's ability to create more dynamic and diverse cultures.

2.1 Physical Appearance and Attributes

Physical appearance is an outward display of a person's attributes that are visible to others. An individual's physical appearance is the most common way other people identify them. A state driver's license customarily includes a photograph of the licensee so that distinctive physical features are evident enough to help identify the person.

Some examples of attributes that describe a person's physical appearance include:

- eye color
- hair color
- weight

- height

- body style or shape or size (such as lanky or muscular)

- a description of body parts (such as a small nose or almond-shaped eyes)

Typically, a person's physical appearance is also the first way a person will attempt to identify someone else. Crimes involving persons, accidents, celebrity sightings, and other situations that rely on a descriptive narrative to identify a person are based on physical appearance or attributes.

Sometimes, a person's physical appearance is devised by choice. People can choose to color their hair, wear contact lenses that change or mask a natural eye color, alter fashion options, and even augment their body features to promote a specific physical appearance. Wearing high-heeled shoes helps to augment a person's height. Waist trainers are designed to give a physical appearance that minimizes the circumference of a person's waistline, torso, or mid-region. These are all appearance alterations that are made by choice. Other physical characteristics are not as easily altered or changed. They can include a person's skin color or physical disabilities that are not altered or modified with aids or other devices.

A person's physical appearance is a part of their identity and subsequently an element of their diversity. Physical attributes are a consistent theme in discrimination, harassment, bias, and racism. As you continue reading, you will learn more about ways in which the diversity of physical characteristics affects how individuals are perceived in the workplace.

2.2 Physical and Mental Abilities

Physical ability is not the same as physical appearance. **Physical ability** refers to a person's ability to perform some type of physical activity. Strength, coordination, balance, dexterity, flexibility, and stamina are all examples of physical ability.

Think about jobs that require a specific physical ability. For example, most athletes must have the physical ability to perform their job successfully. Although there are professional and other sports teams that inclusively embrace individuals with physical disabilities, in general, a sports athlete must still possess particular physical abilities. Other jobs that require some level of physical ability for performance include dancers, warehouse workers, sanitation workers, waiters, construction workers, and many others.

A person's characteristics or identifying traits that cause an inability to perform physical actions, such as the examples listed above, are often referred to as a disability. A **physical disability** is a condition that negatively affects a person's stamina, dexterity, mobility, or physical capacity. There is a wide range of physical disabilities, and each can vary in intensity, severity or lasting effect over time. Physical disabilities can range from conditions like hearing impairment, blindness, and cerebral palsy, to paralysis.

A mental disability is not the same as a mental disorder. It is also separate and distinct from a physical disability. **Mental disability** is when a person does not or cannot develop cognitively at the same rate as most other people. A mentally disabled individual may feel challenged by their ability or capacity to complete tasks, learn or retain information, comprehend simple to complex concepts, or take action based on cognitive function.

Employees at all levels may have physical or mental disabilities that inhibit their capacity to perform in certain positions. Ability level is an example of diversity among individuals in general and at work. Several laws and policies have been put into place to address work-related discrimination, biases, and unfair treatment of individuals with disabilities. The Americans with Disabilities Act (ADA) was enacted to protect individuals with physical or mental disabilities from discrimination. As you cover other sections of this book, additional information about ADA and other laws will be introduced and explained further.

Diversity, including consideration of individuals with disabilities, helps strengthen an organization's talent pool. Simply having a physical or mental disability does not imply that individuals do not have a myriad of other talents, skills, or abilities. Remember the examples about the iceberg, Superman, and unseen elements of a person's identity? It is much more beneficial to seek employees who may have different mental or physical traits that are diverse from the majority of others to access far-reaching potential.

2.3 Sex and Gender

Earlier, you learned that a doctor most often assigns a person's sex at birth. It is important to understand the difference between sex and gender so that individuals in the workplace can express their concerns and needs appropriately. Employees and others may experience adverse effects of specific policies, rules, or expectations in the workplace based on their gender, sex, or the assumptions thereof.

In the workplace, employees will encounter diverse genders and/or sexes. Certain areas within the work environment, such as restrooms, lactation or feeding rooms, and locker rooms are often designated according to one's sex. Male-Female or Man-Woman signs are prevalent throughout many organizations and often can become a point of conflict when policies related to sex and gender, including gender identity, are not addressed appropriately. A person's gender identity helps them express an element of their identity. What are the potential effects of not being aware or understanding the difference between an individual's sex, gender, or gender identity?

Figure 2.1

Set of Restroom vector sign By olando – Adobe Stock File #:264893251

An individual's sex is usually categorized as male or female and most often based on specific biological features like reproductive organs, hormones, genes, and chromosomes. However, biological attributes that determine a specific sex are not binary and can vary.

Initially, scientists and physicians determined that the X and Y chromosomes could identify a person's sex as male or female when they were born. The X and Y chromosomes are sometimes referred to as sex chromosomes because they contribute to how a person's sex develops. Traditionally, females were identified as having two X chromosomes (XX), while males were noted as having one X and one Y chromosome (XY).

Newer and recent studies provide additional information to indicate that X and Y chromosomes alone are not sufficient to determine a baby's sex. Studies have confirmed chromosome variations for both men and women. In some cases, girls and women had XY chromosomes, and boys and men displayed nontypical distinctions as well. For example, a girl with androgen insensitivity syndrome can have XY chromosomes. This syndrome can occur when a gene on the Y chromosome ends up on an X chromosome, causing that X chromosome to function more like a Y.

For clarity, most concur that while genes or chromosomes contribute to development, they do not inherently dictate the gender identity of boys, girls, men, or women.

When reproductive organs look or act differently due to variations, it signifies a difference in sex development, and those differences are sometimes referred to as **intersex**.

Science and medicine now support that being a man or a woman or intersex is a matter of gender identity, not simply one tied to biological features. As you continue with the text, you will learn more about gender identity and its significance in the workplace.

Society uses assigned sex as one of the primary attributes to describe individuals. The characteristic is often included on legal and formal documents like a state-issued license and used to identify someone.

Gender and sex are different. However, neither of them is binary. Biological and genetic make-up help define a person's sex, and **gender** refers to how a person internally identifies and externally expresses themself. External expressions of gender identity can be made using clothing appearances and behaviors. Socially constructed roles of femininity associated with women and masculinity associated with men, behaviors, expressions, and identities also influence the perception of one's gender. However, these social constructs can vary culturally and are not sufficient to determine gender identity. Further, gender role assumptions can often be harmful, toxic, and discriminatory.

According to the medical industry, and medical author, Karthik Kumar, MBBS, more specifically, there are four traditionally recognized genders that apply to living and nonliving objects. The genders include masculine (indicating male subtype), feminine (indicating female subtype), neuter, and common.

Later, we will explore gender more intricately as we discover that many individuals experience and identify with a different gender than their assigned sex at birth. This experience of internal identification and external expression is often represented in the transgender or LGBTQIA+ community, where gender identity becomes even more significant when discussing diversity in the workplace. Chapter six will provide definitions and increase awareness concerning various genders.

2.4 Age

Age is an evident component of diversity. Specific industries or roles may inherently seem more befitting for individuals of one age group versus another. For example, imagine attending a family outing at a local waterpark. Would it be surprising if every employee at the waterpark was over the age of sixty? What about each employee being under the age of twenty? Would it make a difference if the positions were all lifeguards instead of all senior management? Now consider a Fortune 500 company with hundreds of employees, based in a metropolitan area, with a high-rise facility as its headquarters. Would it seem odd if each executive of the organization was under eighteen years old?

People make inferences, have opinions, and often express their sentiments about what age should look like within a company. Sometimes it varies based on industry, and sometimes the position dictates the perception bestowed on the individual in the role.

Surprisingly, age diversity is something that employees are exposed to daily. Depending on the culture, company, clients, customers, or expectations for the position, such diversity can lead to discrimination or harassment that targets both younger and older individuals. Valuing age diversity provides organizations with an opportunity to develop and learn exponentially.

Studies conducted over the decades have attempted to identify and broadly categorize workers based on behavioral characteristics, traits, and attitudes toward work. The chart below identifies five age categories and associated traits for each. The chart is not all-inclusive. However, the information is based on years of data collection, including surveys, observations, inferences, and other information. It can help companies, managers, and others understand potential workplace sentiments, reactions, and behaviors better, based on broad age groups.

Figure 2.2

	Maturists pre-1945	Babyboomers 1945-1960	Generation X 1961-1980	Generation Y 1981-1995	Generation Z born after 1995
aspiration	Home ownership	Job Security	Work-Life balance	Freedom & Flexibility	Security & Stability
attitude toward technology	largely disengaged	early IT adaptors	digital immigrants	digital natives	technoholics
attitude toward career	jobs are for life	careers are defined by employers	loyal to profession, not to employer	work 'with' organization not 'for'	career multitaskers
signature product	car	television	personal computer	smartphone	nano-computing, 3-D print, driverless cars
communication media	formal letter	telephone	e-mail and SMS	SMS or social media	hand-held devices

Generations By desdemona72 – Adobe Stock File #:319695074

Most recently, Mark McCrindle, founder of the Australian consultancy firm McCrindle Research, coined the term, "Generation Alpha." This sixth group includes individuals born from 2010 and after. Generation Alpha is most affectionately characterized by a reliance on technology and a lack of dependency on physical contact with peers. This growing generation is diverse in lifestyles, perspectives, and tastes, and it is all typically represented in the group's independent decision-making and managing their digital identities.

In a work environment, the generation of tech-savvy workers may struggle with having a shorter attention span, decreased concentration, and less development of creativity and imagination as they are accustomed to quick access and information scanning for knowledge. Also, persons in this category may find that socializing outside of their comfort zone consisting of social networks, is bothersome.

Managers and supervisors who tap into the variances between generations concerning age diversity will likely benefit from an increased understanding of employee aspirations, attitudes toward career endeavors, communication preferences, and more. Such enlightenment will help to identify resolutions to challenges that may have previously seemed impossible to address.

There are no global or universal rules dictating the age at which individuals may begin working. However, minimum age requirements vary from industry to industry or for specific roles to ensure safety, legality, and other aspects directly impacting an individual, organization, or industry. In some instances, child labor laws in different states and nations are enacted and designed to protect children's rights and support parental or guardianship approval of child workers.

Similarly, there are no global or universal rules indicating a maximum age at which an individual may work. However, some industries and organizations may lawfully impose restrictions on age, preventing individuals from working in specific capacities.

In most cases and most industries, maximum age restrictions are not lawful. Labor laws, rules, and policies are often implemented to protect older workers from discriminatory practices in hiring, promotions, and other aspects of work beneficial to the employee.

Organizations that create or follow policies or practices that harm applicants or employees over a certain age can be illegal if the policy is not based on a reasonable factor other than age. In the United States, The Age Discrimination in Employment Act

(ADEA) forbids age discrimination against people age 40 or older. The same protection is not afforded to workers under age 40. This type of discrimination also applies if both the victim and the person inflicting the discrimination are over 40. ADEA prohibits discrimination in any aspect of employment, including hiring, firing, pay, job assignments, promotions, layoff, training, benefits, and any other terms or conditions of employment.

2.5 Race, Ethnicity and Nationality

Race, ethnicity, and nationality are three distinct categories that help establish one's identity. They are additional elements of what uniquely makes one individual or group diverse from others. Each of the three categories helps classify individuals into broader distinct populations or groups. It is critical to understand the difference between the three identifiers because each plays a key role in ensuring diversity, equity, and inclusion in the workplace. Also, failure to understand the distinction between each may cause employers, coworkers, supervisors, or others to misinterpret an individual's self-proclaimed identity. Remember that a person's identity is quite significant to how they live and work. It affects their daily lives and is a part of them that they carry with them to work.

When elements of identity in the workplace are not acknowledged appropriately, it may give the impression that they are not important or desirable. In order to embrace diversity through identity, it is critical to understand, acknowledge, and accept how individuals are identified, portrayed, or perceived regarding race, ethnicity, and nationality.

Race

Race is central to identity and diversity, as it is based on large classifications of individuals who share distinct anatomical or physical characteristics like skin color. Many scientists still debate whether race is a biological construct or not.

According to the U.S. Census Bureau and U.S. Office of Management and Budget (OMB), a relatively short list of racial categories is used for identification purposes. OMB states that "the racial categories included in the census questionnaire generally reflect a social definition of race recognized in this country [the U.S.] and not an attempt to define race biologically, anthropologically, or genetically... people may choose to report more than one race to indicate their racial mixture."

The [six] groups that make up the categories for census data collection include White, Black or African American, American Indian or Alaska Native, Asian, Native Hawaiian or Other Pacific Islander, and Some Other Race. The final category allows respondents to select or report more than one race.

Persons who identify as Spanish, Latino, or Hispanic may be considered any race, as those identifiers are not considered a race but rather an ethnicity. The OMB uses the following to define race categories:

- **White** - A person having origins in any of the original peoples of Europe, the Middle East, or North Africa. It includes people who indicate their race as "White" or report entries such as Irish, German, Italian, Lebanese, Arab, Moroccan, or Caucasian.

- **Black or African American** - A person having origins in any of the Black racial groups of Africa. It includes people who indicate their race as "Black or African American" or report entries such as African American, Kenyan, Nigerian, or Haitian.

- **American Indian and Alaska Native** - A person having origins in any of the original peoples of North and South America (including Central America) and who maintains tribal affiliation or community attachment. This category includes people who indicate their race as "American Indian or Alaska Native" or report entries such as Navajo, Blackfeet, Inupiat, Yup'ik, Central American Indian groups, or South American Indian groups.

- **Asian** - A person having origins in any of the original peoples of the Far East, Southeast Asia, or the Indian subcontinent, including, for example, Cambodia, China, India, Japan, Korea, Malaysia, Pakistan, the Philippine Islands, Thailand, and Vietnam. This includes people who reported detailed Asian responses such as: "Asian Indian," "Chinese," "Filipino," "Korean," "Japanese," "Vietnamese," and "Other Asian" or provide other detailed Asian responses.

- **Native Hawaiian and Other Pacific Islander** - A person having origins in any of the original peoples of Hawaii, Guam, Samoa, or other Pacific Islands. It includes people who reported their race as "Fijian," "Guamanian or Chamorro," "Marshallese," "Native Hawaiian," "Samoan," "Tongan," and "Other Pacific Islander" or provide other detailed Pacific Islander responses.

Individuals may choose to self-identify as two or more races either by checking two or more boxes, by providing multiple responses, or by some combination of checkboxes and other responses.

Many people assume that a person's race is indicative of their ethnicity or origin. However, skin color or biological construct is not sufficient to make such a conclusion. Race is indicative of biological linkage expressing variations within the linkage. Scientists purport that a person can never alter their race because it is a biological subspecies with a foundation in DNA.

Some anthropologists believe there is more genetic variation within one particular race than between different races. The African American race is often used as an example of morphological feature variation due to the distinct diversity in skin tone, facial structure, complexion, and other biological features within the race itself. Still, race indicates a population that has anatomical resemblance among its members.

Adversely, some sociologists consider race a social construct rather than a biological one. Skin color, when used to determine race, aided in oppression, slavery, and conquest. Without such social constructs tied to race, it would prove much more difficult to make racial distinctions solely on an individual's physical appearance.

Ethnicity

Although often used interchangeably, race and ethnicity are different. **Ethnicity** refers to shared language, ancestry, religion, heritage, or belonging to a social group with common natural or cultural traditions or customs. Customs and traditions that are exclusive to specific regions or geographic locations help to tell the story of where individuals are from. Ethnicity can be characterized by religion, food patterns, style of dress, and other characteristics.

Consider a child born in India to two Asian-Indian parents. Both parents identify with the Asian race and Asian-Indian culture, including speaking the Hindi language. If the child is adopted as a toddler into a Russian family who lives in Russia, the child may eventually identify with a different ethnicity than that of his birth parents. The child will likely grow up identifying with Russian culture, an East Slavic ethnic group native to Eastern Europe. As a toddler, not yet having established a full understanding of the Hindi language or conforming to the Asian-Indian culture, his race is not significant enough to form a complete identity of his ethnic background or upbringing. However, because of his acclimation and exposure to Russian culture, the child may feel Russian. He may eat foods unique to the region or culture, speak Russian, or even engage in traditions and practices associated with the ethnicity.

The child's physical and biological attributes, helping to identify his race, will always be a factor in how he is viewed and likely treated by society when interacting with the world. As the child continues to grow and simply present himself physically, it is more likely that the impression of others will be to conclude that he is of Asian-Indian descent and therefore identifies with the Asian-Indian culture or ethnicity. However, it would become immediately apparent as he begins to express elements of his identity through food preference, dress, language, and other elements, that his ethnicity is quite different from his race.

Therefore, a primary distinction between race and ethnicity is that race has biological variations between groups and ethnicity indicates cultural and traditional variations.

Individuals can choose to become a member of an ethnic group. Conforming to shared religious, cultural, or other practices within a group is indicative of ethnicity. Subsequently, the number of ethnic groups worldwide is significantly greater than racial categories.

Sometimes race and ethnicity overlap. For example, an African-Asian person may consider themselves a member of either the African or Asian race independently. However, if the individual does not engage in any of the customs, traditions, or ancestorial practices typically associated with either race, then they are not identifying with the ethnicity or conforming to it. Subsequently, the individual may choose one ethnic identity over the other, or even a third one not associated with their race. Individuals may also have a mixed ethnic background, where each parent is from a different ethnic background and the person embraces, conforms to, or identifies with both ethnicities.

Figure 2.3

RACE
VERSUS
ETHNICITY

Race is considered to be a biological classification	Ethnicity is considered to be a cultural identity
Can sometimes be determined by the physical appearance	Can sometimes be determined by the manner of dressing
Member of one race cannot join another race	Member of one ethnicity can join another ethnicity

Image from Pedia.com

Various types of ethnic groups can be formed depending on the source of group identity. They may include just a few to thousands of members. Some variations in ethnic groups include:

- Ethno-racial groups (Ex: Afro-Brazilians)
- Ethnoreligious groups (Ex: Sikhs)
- Ethnonational groups (Ex: Pakistani)
- Ethnolinguistic (Ex: Gaels)

Nationality

Nationality is a legal construct referring to a person's relationship with the country or nation where they were born, live in, or hold citizenship. It is mainly influenced by geographical location and political boundaries. In law, nationality affords the state jurisdiction over a person and ensures he or she is protected by the state.

The main difference between ethnicity and nationality is that while ethnicity is a social construct, nationality is a legal construct.

An individual who has lived in France for many years may consider herself French. However, her ethnicity might be African. Similarly, consider an Australian who has been granted citizenship and has been living in China for many years might consider his nationality to be Chinese.

2.6 Status

A person's **status** is their rank, standing, position, or state compared to others in society, groups, or organizations. People can have different statuses in society and other environments like work. For example, upper and middle classes are both descriptive of a person's financial status. There are other societal statuses related to the rights, duties, and lifestyle in a social hierarchy based upon honor or prestige. Describing a person as a member of the clergy, for example, indicates a particular status.

The work environment also has individuals whose status dictates how a person is perceived. The significance of status directly relates to diversity in the workplace. At work, status is used to diversify levels in an organization. For example, Chief of Staff, executive, shareholder, or owner can all describe a person's rank or position in an organization. Those statuses are perceived as higher ranking than other positions like a designer, salesman, engineer, recruiter, or manager.

Unfortunately, status can also have an adverse impact in the workplace. Some individuals view status as an indicator of the amount of respect, honor, or trust that should be granted to a person. Consider a small to medium-sized company. The company may only have a few employees, one of whom is the owner or founder. Most people immediately identify an owner as being in a position of authority or having power. The status helps define how others perceive the owner's ability to exercise such power, thus ensuring they are respectful in their communication with or about the individual. Similarly, in larger organizations, employees may work in close proximity with individuals in various positions and at different levels. The hierarchy within the organization or team denotes a specific status for different people.

Perception of Status

Imagine someone who finally got a chance to interview for a long-sought-after position. Upon entering a large plush office building, the interviewee encounters an individual on the elevator, standing with a bucket of soapy water and a mop. The individual on the elevator speaks to the interviewee. However, the interviewee is focused on his appointment and what he will say during the interview and disregards the greeting made by the person on the elevator. The interviewee does not return the greeting and seemingly ignores the individual.

Upon stepping off the elevator, the interviewee sees a sign and walks toward a receptionist on the floor where he plans to interview. The interviewee steps up to the desk and informs the receptionist that he is there to meet with the company's owner. After the interviewee mentions who he is there to meet, the receptionist smiles and says, "I'm surprised you didn't meet him in the elevator. He typically speaks to everyone who enters the building. He just exited the elevator with you and headed toward his office."

> **Reflection – Perception of Status**
>
> 1. How do you think the interviewee would react?
>
> 2. What reasons might the interviewee have for failing to speak to the person in the elevator?
>
> 3. What do you think the man with the bucket and mop thought about the interviewee?
>
> 4. Could the interviewee have assumed that the individual on the elevator did not have the status of someone in the organization in a position of power or authority?
>
> 5. Several factors could have caused the interviewee to perceive the owner's status as something different than his actual status. What factors do you think made a difference in the interviewee's perception?
>
> 6. Would the interaction have been different if it were a smaller company like a single-story restaurant or convenience store, where the owner's status was not immediately discernible?

An individual's status in the workplace should help identify structural levels within a company and not be used to disregard, discriminate, disadvantage, or disrespect any person. Recognizing diversity in status helps to ensure appropriate interaction for working-relationship roles but also opens the door for ensuring equitable, fair, just, and respectful treatment of all individuals within the work environment.

Company structures can vary greatly. Some organizational reporting structures include:

- Traditional vertical reporting structure
- Functional reporting structure

- Divisional or product reporting structure
- Line-and-staff reporting structure
- Flat reporting structure
- Matrix reporting structure
- Network organization structures

Although reporting may vary in each organization, it is critical to ensure respectful and considerate treatment of all individuals regardless of status.

2.7 Language and Communication

Language is one of the features that sets the human species apart from other species on earth. It is how humans communicate with each other and form complex cultures and civilizations.

We learned earlier that individuals have diverse backgrounds and ethnicities. Language and communication in an organization are not simply limited to different world languages or dialects. A person's language is a part of their ethnicity. Some individuals speak multiple languages, and within those languages, there may be diversity in the dialect also.

Language or linguistic diversity describes the differences between different languages and the ways that people communicate with each other.

It is imperative to acknowledge and respect individuals who speak the same, similar, or different languages from oneself in a company. Often, organizations value such diversity as it equips the company with a human resource who is able to interact with a larger and more diverse customer base. Many companies recruit specifically for individuals who speak multiple languages. Job ads or postings may read similar to the following: "Seeking an English/Spanish bi-lingual associate with exceptional customer service skills."

Types of Linguistic Diversity

At work, and even in other environments, there are several situations where people may have diverse linguistic expressions and needs. These situations present pros and cons for everyone involved in the communication.

Types of linguistic diversity include:

Table 2.1

Type of Linguistic Diversity	Description	Ways to Address Linguistic Diversity at Work
English language learners (ELLs) or English as a Second Language (ESL)	Individuals learning English as a second language, usually where most others are native English speakers	ELLs may need differentiated learning strategies but can also bring cultural and linguistic enrichment to the work environment; Customers, clients, and other stakeholders may benefit from communication with individuals who speak the same native language
Sign languages	Individuals who are d/Deaf, hard of hearing, and who may use American Sign Language (ASL) or other sign languages as a primary communication	Employees who are deaf or hard of hearing may need accommodations at work, and employee training on language and linguistic diversity may help to improve inclusion, understanding, and acceptance for all employees
Speech disorders	Aphasia, apraxia, stuttering, selective mutism, and others	Speech disorders are relatively common. Employee training to celebrate rather than stigmatizing a wide variety of speech styles may prove beneficial in the workplace.

A **language diversity index** measures linguistic diversity. It identifies the likelihood of two people in a region who speak the same native language. When almost everyone in a region speaks the same language, the diversity index will approach 0, indicating that there is not much diversity in the language spoken among the people. Contrarily, a high degree of native language diversity causes the index to approach 1.

A few countries with a low diversity index of 0.2 or less include Britain, Brazil, Australia, and Japan. The U.S. also has a relatively low index, with a score between 0.2 and 0.4. Countries with a very high diversity index of 0.8 or higher include South Africa (11 official languages), India, and Papua New Guinea.

High levels of linguistic diversity often indicate that a country has one or more of the following:

- A vast population
- Many ethnic groups
- Many historical and current trade routes
- A history of being colonized
- Many mountains and other isolating geographical features

Reflecting on what you learned about race, ethnicity, and nationality, it may now seem more obvious why certain regions or countries have higher linguistic diversity than others.

Applying the knowledge of language, communication, and language diversity in the workplace helps to foster more inclusive, accepting, and trusting relationships. Dialect, accents, and other variations in language can often present barriers to effective working relationships. Learning to value and understand the inherent nature of a person's language and communication needs allows room for individual and organizational growth. Once language is explored as an element of diversity, it can also be leveraged to form stronger teams, cultures, and companies.

2.8 Spirituality and Religion

A person's spirituality or religion may be influenced by several factors, including their ethnicity, nationality, or mere desire to affiliate with or join specific religious organizations or groups. Individuals may identify with, celebrate, or embrace different religions in their personal lives. These religions and beliefs do not cease to exist when a person goes to work. However, certain practices, traditions, or customs may be suppressed, inappropriate, or misunderstood if exercised in a work environment.

Some organizations may require that individuals conform to a specific religion. For example, ministers, clergy members, or even staff employees of a religious organization may require all employees to subscribe to the same or similar beliefs of the organization as a whole. However, in other work environments, such as law enforcement, medicine, or other industries where the entire company is not affiliated with a single religion or belief, it may be highly inappropriate to engage in practices or traditions related to religion or spirituality while at work.

There are thousands of religions around the world. At work, it is important to know that although not all religious practices are acceptable, a company or its employees should not judge, criticize, ridicule, or disrespect an individual's beliefs. Accepting an individual's right or desire to believe in or practice a particular religion is not the same as accepting the religion for oneself.

Religion is a part of a person's identity. It is not fair, just, or appropriate to encourage identity expression through religion for some while oppressing the same for others. The key is to accept religious diversity among all individuals rather than embrace or attempt only to accept those that conform to one's own beliefs.

2.9 Socioeconomic Background

Socioeconomic background comprises a person's income, occupation, and social background. It is often considered a key determinant of success and future life chances. When employees assume roles and responsibilities at work, it is not inherently indicative of their income. There are instances where assumptions may be made. For example, if an individual takes occupation in a position that pays minimum wage for the role, it may appear that they were not born into a wealthy family or have a high personal income. However, this perception is not fact and can be misleading.

Individuals take different jobs for different reasons. Sometimes the reason is for the pay rate or wage that the individual will earn. That rate can indicate the level of education that a person has attained. For example, it may be challenging to secure a high-level engineering position for someone who has not attained a secondary education in mathematics, engineering, science, or a related field. However, it is not impossible to secure such a role even if someone has never been to college.

Similarly, a person who accepts a position in a highly compensated role may or may not have previously had a background, income, or social status where they were highly compensated. Their socioeconomic background, therefore, is not the sole indicator of their aptitude for success in a role.

The work environment is full of individuals with diverse socioeconomic backgrounds. Similar to other elements of diversity, employers and others must refrain from assumptions related to such a status that may lead to inequity or lack of inclusion.

2.10 Learning Style

There are more things to learn about the world, the people in it, and how it all works together than the capacity for one individual to comprehend it all. Every person is uniquely distinct from the next in one way or another. Whether it is race, age, gender, sex, ethnicity, or any other element of diversity, there will inevitably be a difference between individuals. Similarly, there are distinct differences between groups of people.

Ethnicity, race, nationality, status, and working generation are among a few of the diverse elements that describe how groups differ from each other. These broad groups suggest that the individuals within them share something in common. **Learning style** describes the style or modality in which individuals prefer to learn or are capable of learning. It is also a characteristic that individuals have separately, but that can be categorized collectively.

Four modalities reflect how people learn. The acronym **VARK** stands for Visual, Aural, Reflective (reading/writing), and Kinesthetic sensory modalities used for learning information. These are the styles in which people absorb and retain information.

Employees may also prefer a primary modality for learning. Employers who understand that training and development require flexibility to accommodate the various learning styles within the workplace will find that ensuring flexibility for diverse learners also produces a benefit. Some employees will grasp information, content, and concepts differently than others, and in some cases, utilize the information differently to benefit the organization or team.

Figure 2.4

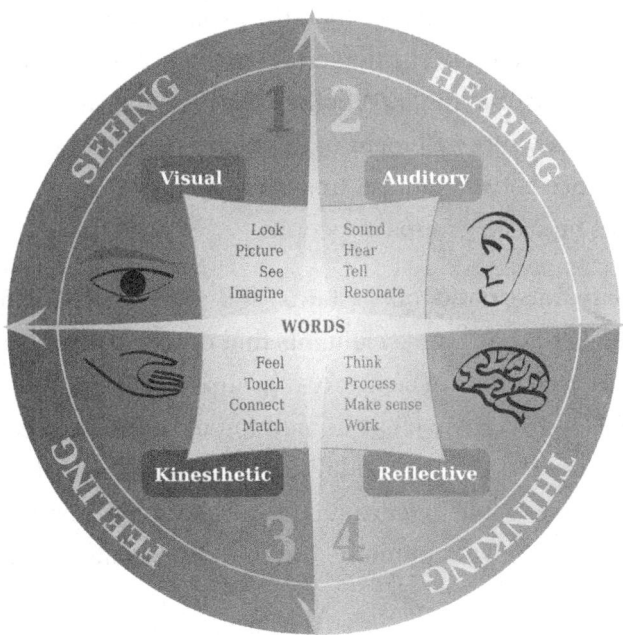

Diagramme 4 Styles Apprentissage / Communication - NLP – Coach By Artellia – AdobeStock File #:91055299

Visual (V):

Learners prefer depictions of information in maps, designs, whitespace, patterns, shapes, symbols, diagrams, charts, graphs, flow charts, hierarchies, and other devices that people use to represent what could have been presented in words. This preference does not include still or motion pictures, PowerPoint, or photographs.

Aural / Auditory (A):

Learners prefer to receive information that is heard or spoken. Optimal delivery forms include lectures, group discussion, radio, phones, speaking, web-chat, and talking things through. The Aural preference includes talking aloud, talking to oneself, or sorting things out by speaking first. Learners may repeat what has already been said or ask an obvious and previously answered question. Learners need to hear and then say it their way.

Reflective (read/write) (R):

Learners prefer information displayed as words. This preference emphasizes reading and writing in all its forms. Ideally, learners grasp more from manuals, reports, essays, and assignments. People who prefer this modality often thrive using PowerPoint, the Internet, lists, diaries, quotes, books, and written resources like dictionaries.

Kinesthetic (K):

People who prefer this mode are connected to reality and touch and learn through concrete personal experiences. Demonstrations, examples, simulation, practice, videos, and movies of "real" things, as well as case studies, are all optimal solutions for kinesthetic learning.

Multimodality (MM):

Many people do not have a standout mode or a preference for a single learning style. They learn equally or better from using multiple modes. A preference for a particular mode does not imply that a person can only learn using that particular style or that other modes are ineffective.

When employers attain new talent and deliver orientations or training programs, they should always remain aware of the diversity among the learners. Valuing such diversity will help promote a more efficient knowledge transfer and build stronger connections between companies and employees.

2.11 Working Style

Have you ever noticed that some people at work move quickly, seemingly operating with a complete purpose for every movement and rarely stopping to say hello to others around them? Other people may seem to stroll or never rush to get from one place to the next while casually speaking to anyone in their path. These differences are not merely distinctions in how quickly someone moves from their office to the boardroom or from a meeting to the breakroom. They are also indicative of a person's nature and how they perceive themselves and expectations at work.

At work, people function differently from each other. A person's **working style** is essentially the way they go about their day-to-day tasks on the job. The method that people employ allows them to perform to the best of their abilities. Forcing individuals to work in a manner that is not conducive to their inherent behavior can sometimes backfire or make their work harder.

For example, many job ads include a note that the company is seeking a team player. Being a team player does not necessarily mean being capable of performing on a team project. Some individuals are more inclined to work independently than work within groups or teams. The desire for such independence does not, however, imply that they are not collaborative, willing to share or give information, or that they are standoffish with others. It may simply imply that a person's work style or preference requires solitude.

Some people may feel more efficient when working independently and responsible for their own schedule and tasks. Others require a collaborative group environment, strongly influenced by set tasks, deadlines, and deliverables. These are situations where work styles vary.

Some examples of descriptive characteristics of work styles include:

- Adaptable
- Collaborative
- Confident
- Creative
- Detail-oriented
- Flexible
- Focused
- Independent
- Motivated
- Organized, and
- Reliable

Some workers thrive using lists, coordinating, and planning while checking off little boxes related to tasks that need to be completed. Others may feel buried and overwhelmed because they need more flexibility and creativity in their movements and day-to-day accomplishments. Neither of these ways can be classified as right or wrong. Nevertheless, they are an element of diversity that sometimes can be misconstrued in the workplace.

Type A individuals may consider Type B personalities as uncommitted or chatty. Type B personalities may think Type A personalities have too much structure or do not know how to balance social engagement within the workplace effectively. These examples of how personalities influence workstyles can often conflict among teams and create issues with synergy and subsequent work output. It is essential to understand various work styles and equally important to embrace all of them.

2.12 Talents, Skills, and Aptitude

The world of work is vast. Just like there is diversity in individuals, there are hundreds of industries and thousands of professions. Each role or position is different from others in one way or another. Professionals like singers, artists, musicians, actors, managers, engineers, authors, and delivery drivers all have something in common. Each professional has a specific set of skills or talents that enable them to perform in their selected role.

Of course, not everyone is exceptional at their job. Not everyone excels to a level where they are given accolades or substantial pay or benefits for what they do. However, each person has an aptitude to succeed at their work. Often that aptitude is enhanced by skills, talents, desire to grow, and innate abilities tied to physical or mental capacity.

One of the most desirable elements of diversity for organizations should be the skill or talent a person brings to a role. The minimum qualifications for a position typically outline years of experience, educational criteria, or certification. However, preferred qualifications usually delve into abilities such as comprehension of subjects or coachability.

Companies who pursue diverse candidates based on talents, skills, and aptitude rather than diversity based on physical characteristics will find a greater advantage for leveraging the value of diversity. Recruiting candidates based on different talent levels, skills and aptitude does not imply that corporations only seek individuals who have already attained high levels. Sometimes an organization's goal is to train, develop and grow their talent from the skill at which the employee entered the organization to greater skills.

Training, development, mentoring, and coaching are all aspects of how an organization should approach talent and performance management. Relying only on highly skilled employees decreases the value of diversity where lesser-skilled employees may have otherwise received an opportunity to grow and develop in an organization or role. Similarly, only seeking candidates or employees with a specific talent eliminates the ability to find exceptional employees who may be highly skilled in one area and trainable in another.

2.12.1 EQ and IQ

EQ and IQ are acronyms for two different terms that are often confused mistakenly used interchangeably. **IQ** stands for Intelligence Quotient and measures a person's relative intelligence. **EQ** stands for Emotional Quotient and represents the ability to identify and manage, evaluate, control, and express one's emotions and the emotions of others.

Whereas IQ is used to determine academic abilities and identify individuals with exceptional intelligence or mental challenges, EQ demonstrates the ability to achieve success in the workplace and identifies leaders, good team players, and people who best work by themselves. EQ can help gauge an employee's mood, their emotional state, and understand their reactions and weaknesses better.

Table 2.2   EQ versus IQ comparison Chart

	EQ	IQ
Stands for	Emotional Quotient (aka emotional intelligence)	Intelligence Quotient
In the workplace	Teamwork, leadership, successful relations, service orientation, initiative, collaboration.	Success with challenging tasks, ability to analyze and connect the dots, research, and development.
Identifies	Leaders, team players, individuals who best work alone, individuals with social challenges.	Highly capable or gifted individuals, individuals with mental challenges and special needs.

"EQ vs. IQ." Diffen.com. by Kate T., Gauri S., Nikhilesh Jasuja.

Quiz

1. Todd is a talent scout for a marketing company. He is in charge of recruiting talent for print ads, commercials, and other productions. One of the company's clients is a retirement facility for seniors. Which of the following types of diversity is Todd least likely to seek when recruiting talent for print ads for the retirement facility?

    a. Race, Ethnicity, and Nationality

    b. Sex and Gender

    c. Age and Physical Disability

    d. Spirituality and Religion, and Language

2. Which types of diversity should employers embrace? Select all that apply.

    a. Age, Gender, and Socioeconomic background

    b. Race, Physical Ability/Disability, and Learning style

    c. Language, Sex, and Emotional Intelligence

    d. A and B

    e. All of the Above

3. Which of the following is False concerning race and ethnicity?

    a. Ethnicity is a biological classification.

    b. A person of one ethnicity can become a member of a different ethnicity.

    c. A person of a particular race cannot become a member of a different race.

    d. Ethnicity is a part of one's cultural identity.

4. According to the acronym VARK, which of the following is not descriptive of the various modalities for learning?

    a. Auditory

    b. Repetition

    c. Kinesthetic

    d. Reflective

    e. Visual

5. **Of the following answer choices, which best demonstrates ways organizations can create more diverse cultures?**

   a. Recruit talent with similar beliefs, values, and goals as the organization to build stability.

   b. Avoid hiring individuals with criminal backgrounds or poor work history.

   c. Consider aspects of diversity that may have traditionally been overlooked.

   d. Create more programs for older employees.

| Answers | 1 – d | 2 – e | 3 – a | 4 – b | 5 – c |

*Detailed Explanation to the above questions can be downloaded from the **Online Resources** section of this book on www.vibrantpublishers.com*

Chapter Summary

- Diversity is everything about the human race that makes one individual or group different from another.

- Certain aspects of diversity have traditionally been overlooked, disregarded, or unknown.

- Physical appearance is typically the first way people identify others.

- Individuals can have physical and mental disabilities.

- Sex and gender are different. Sex is based on biological features and gender refers to how a person identifies internally and expresses themself externally.

- Discrimination based on age diversity in the workplace can be targeted at younger or older individuals.

- Race, ethnicity, and nationality are different. Race is based on physical characteristics, ethnicity is based on shared customs or cultural traditions, and nationality is a legal construct referring to a person's relationship with a country or region.

- The perception of an individual's status can have an adverse impact in the workplace.

- Language or linguistic diversity describes differences between languages and how people communicate and include sign languages, speech disorders, and English language learners.

- Not all religion or religious practices are appropriate or acceptable in the workplace, but each organization must respect varying employee beliefs .

- Socioeconomic background comprises a person's income, occupation, and social background and is often considered a key determinant of success and future life chances.

- VARK is an acronym to describe the four learning styles: Visual, Auditory, Read/Write, and Kinesthetic. Each style should be embraced to leverage learning potential for employees.

- Working style is how people go about their day-to-day tasks on the job.

- Pursing diverse candidates based on talents, skills and aptitude will provide a greater advantage for leveraging the value of diversity.

- Companies should consider EQ when searching for candidate diversity.

This page is intentionally left blank

Chapter 3

Organizational Culture

Chapter three examines organizational culture and the impact of diversity on the organization's people, processes, practices, and systems. The chapter exposes readers to individual and group behaviors, underlying assumptions, and organizational values that adversely impact workers and the environment. Different levels of organizational culture are presented and examined to demonstrate how each level contributes to building or harming the culture.

Key learning objectives should include the reader's understanding of the following

- Definition of key terms: organizational culture, cultural identity, harassment, discrimination, bias, unconscious bias, sexual harassment, sex-based harassment, microaggressions, employer of choice, hiring practices, recruitment, selection, and artificial intelligence
- The difference between discrimination, harassment, bias, and unconscious bias

- The three levels that define organizational culture
- Various types of unconscious bias
- Awareness and acknowledgment of microaggressions by oneself and others
- Biases in hiring practices and artificial intelligence

Like identity and diversity, culture is a complex notion that comprises many parts. Each organization is a cultural unit that is made up of influential subcultures. Most companies have several people, teams, and groups. The groups are diverse and vary in the reason or method they were formed. Some groups, like accountants or engineers, are defined by the workers' skills. A broader profession, like Human Resources, sales, or law, could also describe a department, team, or group. Other groups may be categorized by the biological, cultural, or self-identifying attributes of individuals within them.

Consider the many different ways groups could be categorized or identified. Teams are made up of unique individuals who each have separate identities. Within a person's identity, there are many characteristics and traits that all govern how the person acts, feels, and believes. Therefore, culture is not only represented by what an individual experiences externally but also by what lies within each person.

Organizational culture is the shared underlying assumptions, behaviors, beliefs, values, and ways of interacting that contribute to an organization's environment. According to Edgar Schein's Culture Framework, culture has three primary levels: artifacts, espoused values, and underlying assumptions. These three levels determine how culture manifests in a company.

Artifacts

The first level of an organization's culture is its artifacts. Artifacts are visible organizational structures and processes. They can be seen, heard, or felt emotionally within the culture. Examples may include office or building décor, symbols, logos, a fast-paced environment, a relaxed dress code, or even employees' mood. An organization's artifacts draw an immediate emotional response from individuals. They give people a sense of what is around them. Closed doors, noisy areas, or extremely quiet conference rooms all represent artifacts of the company. For example, a person interviewing for a bank teller position, dressed in traditional business attire with a suit and tie, may feel an immediate emotional response walking into a bank where the office décor includes paintings of rock groups and images of people dressed in a gothic look. For the interviewee, it may feel like the traditional business model or expected objectives of a bank are misaligned with its décor. The environment or culture could then become a source of confusion for the potential new hire.

Although processes and structures emit energy-invoking emotional responses, artifacts are not sufficient enough to solely describe an organization's culture. Artifacts alone can be hard to decipher, misinterpreted, or misaligned with other parts of the company's culture.

Espoused Values

Many businesses operate under an established vision and mission statement. More thorough organizations also incorporate objectives, strategies, tactics, and goals. A company's espoused values are its strategies, goals, and philosophies, including the vision and mission statement. These elements of the organization are adopted by the individuals within them. The organization's values help paint an even clearer picture of a company and provide individuals with a deeper understanding of its attempt to present itself to employees and others.

Companies, employees, and customers should all be able to determine consistency between artifacts and values. For example, a company should not purport to have a family-first culture yet also have policies that negatively impact employees who take off work to attend medical appointments for children or the funeral of a lost loved one. When a company's artifacts and espoused values do not line up, the deeper cultural level should be examined for clarity concerning the company's culture.

Underlying Assumptions

The underlying assumptions within an organization are the unspoken beliefs, feelings, perceptions, and thoughts of the people within the company. Typically, the values, beliefs, and assumptions of the individual or groups who initially founded the company become ingrained in the organization's culture. Subsequently, those assumptions become a normal and expected part of the culture. The beliefs are passed through behaviors, customs, artifacts, values, and processes that occur within the company. The beliefs are commonly shared and taken for granted as correct or proper. They are not widely questioned and are therefore presumed just to be a part of the organizational culture. Learned, shared, and unquestioned assumptions derived from the culture drive behavior that pours back into the organization's culture, creating a cycle of what is typical or expected.

Figure 3.1   Company Culture Levels

Artifacts	• Visible • Evokes emotional reaction • Hard to decipher
Espoused Values	• Strategies, objectives, philosophies • May appear inconsistent with artifacts (until deeper exploration)
Underlying Assumptions	• Beliefs, feelings, perceptions, thoughts

Understanding organizational culture is vital to embracing diversity within the workplace. A successful organization must have a culture where artifacts, values, and assumptions are aligned and supported by individuals at all company levels. In a strong culture, employees understand expectations and roles and are confident that their responses to circumstances follow the company culture.

Think of a company like a small doctor's office that prides itself on patient or client privacy and confidentiality. A newly hired employee may notice artifacts like signs reminding people of privacy rights, symbolism, or logos promoting confidentiality. She may be aware of the company's mission, goals, or objectives. The employee may be exposed to rigid processes that are designed to protect the privacy of individuals.

In the same company, the employee may find that although many elements of the company's culture are aligned to promote privacy, employees often speak openly and gossip during break time or when off the clock. Although behavior is observable and is an artifact of the company, the behavior seems to be misaligned with the company's values. This inconsistency can present an anomaly for the organizational culture. It may become difficult for employees to decipher the expected behavior or understand their role in building a more robust organizational culture.

Behavioral expectations within an organization are derived from leadership. Leadership relies heavily on espoused values, artifacts, and underlying assumptions to convey a message and brand for their company. Employers who seek to create strong organizational cultures are tasked with reviewing the levels of culture within the company and ensuring they are consistently understood, valued, and perpetuated.

When a company's levels of culture do not incorporate diversity in a manner that allows employees and others to recognize, respond to and nurture it, they must be reevaluated and restructured to ensure proper cultural acceptance and behavior. Employers can begin by incorporating their values into their recruiting, hiring, and onboarding processes so that any values, artifacts, and assumptions are promoted and sustained each time a new individual enters the organization. Employees thus become aware of the expected and proper way to behave within the company.

Cultural identity can vary, and there is no single way to develop a culture that works for all organizations. Instead, each company should determine what and how it wants to be portrayed and work to create shared beliefs and values that are subsequently communicated and reinforced through various methods, ultimately shaping employee perceptions, behaviors, and understanding.

Equally, a cultural identity grounded in inconsistent culture levels can be detrimental to a company and its leadership. Undesirable results such as low employee morale, high turnover, poor customer relations, employee performance issues, and low profits are examples of how a struggling culture can negatively impact the bottom line.

Research evidence shows that two-thirds of company mergers fail because of cultural problems. Blending and redefining the cultures and reconciling the differences builds a more sustainable platform for the future.

3.1 Impact of Diversity on Organizational Culture

Undoubtedly, a part of each organizational culture should be its commitment to diversity. Diversity plays a role in an organization's culture and in helping to define how it is viewed by its employees, clients, customers, and other stakeholders. The workforce should not only be inviting but should be an environment that is conducive enough for employees to feel safe, productive, and welcome.

Employees and others should be able to determine various elements of diversity within the workplace that not only include visible factors but underlying assumptions, typical behaviors, expectations, and the values the company has altogether.

Remember that an individual's identity is a part of them. People feel comfortable when they are welcomed, understood, valued, and appreciated. At work, this means that every aspect of who a person is must be respected and nurtured in order to promote productivity. Productivity relies on performance, and performance suffers when an employee cannot focus on work because they are experiencing other challenging issues within the workplace. The employer has a key role in fostering a high-performance culture, free from stressors that negatively impact employment and performance.

Imagine a work environment where everyone except a single individual is highly educated, each person having a secondary degree or higher, except one individual. Might the individual without the same educational credentials feel overwhelmed, undervalued, or even experience some other levels of discomfort? What about a workplace where only a single person is a female, and the rest of the workforce is male? How about an environment where everyone has the physical capability to perform a function, and a single individual is disabled concerning the specific function? All of these circumstances are elements exposing diversity within the workplace. Each of them is also a circumstance in which diversity can impact the workplace. A worker may not feel relaxed or productive when focusing on diversity issues or if those issues are brought to the forefront more aggressively through actions like bias, harassment, or microaggressions.

Companies should develop and employ strategies that promote a conducive work environment considering various types of diversity within them. When a company demonstrates its commitment to diversity in employees' age, gender, race, educational background, socioeconomic status, gender identity, and the various other areas this book has outlined, the company also infuses specific protection and value for such diversity. Employers, managers, the human resource management, and employees all have an obligation to ensure that employee values and rights in the company are not trampled upon. To accomplish this, a collaborative effort must exist to establish shared values within the company to build and promote a positive organizational culture.

Leaders and companies should devise policies, processes, and artifacts that include and encourage diversity. Employees must perpetuate these values and assumptions and also help to identify when there is a misalignment in the company's desire to promote values and its demonstration of those same values.

Diversity within the workplace can decrease attrition, improve productivity, and solidify social impact, helping companies become employers of choice for various individuals and groups of diverse identities. Therefore, organizations must understand the necessity of creating and managing organizational culture. Later, we will discover processes, technology, and other solutions for building stronger, more diverse cultures.

3.2 Harassment and Discrimination

All employees have a legal right to work in a professional atmosphere free from harassment and discriminatory practices. Concerning the workplace, **harassment** is primarily defined as unwelcome verbal or non-verbal conduct that shows hostility, aggression, or aversion toward another person based on the receiver's protected characteristic(s) and that affects the person's employment. At work, harassment can have the effect of unreasonably interfering with the person's work performance or creating an intimidating, hostile, or offensive working environment. Harassing conduct includes, but is not limited to inappropriate touching and other forms of unwanted sexual contact; epithets; threatening, intimidating, or hostile acts; slurs or negative stereotyping; denigrating jokes and display or circulation in the workplace of written or graphic material that denigrates or shows hostility; or aversion toward an individual or group based on their protected characteristic.

Many companies create policies that prohibit harassment based on race, color, religion, creed, sex, national origin, age, disability, marital status, veteran status, or other status protected by applicable law. Some companies devise more comprehensive policies to incorporate other areas of diversity that may be a target for harassment or discrimination.

Discrimination is an act or behavior based on prejudice and includes, in part, making any employment decision or employment-related action based on race, color, religion, creed, age, sex, disability, national origin, marital or veteran status, or any other status protected by applicable law. **Sexual harassment** is unwelcome sexual advances, requests for sexual favors, and other verbal, visual, or physical conduct of a sexual nature when:

1. Submission to such conduct is made either explicitly or implicitly a term or condition of an individual's employment;

2. Submission to or rejection of such conduct by an individual is used as the basis for employment decisions affecting such individual; or

3. Such conduct has the purpose or effect of unreasonably interfering with an individual's work performance or creating an intimidating, hostile, or offensive working environment.

Sexual harassment can be subtle or overt actions against others by individuals of the same or different genders. Circumstances and situations vary, and behaviors may include but are not limited to: unwelcome or unsolicited sexual advances; unwelcome sexual flirtations, advances, or propositions; suggestive comments; verbal abuse of a sexual nature; displaying sexually suggestive material; sexually-oriented jokes; crude or vulgar language or gestures; display or distribution of obscene materials; graphic or verbal commentaries about an individual's body; physical contact such as patting, pinching or brushing against someone's body; or physical assault of a sexual nature.

Sex-based harassment is not the same as sexual harassment. **Sex-based harassment** does not necessarily involve sexual activity or language but harassment based on an individual's sex or gender. For example, a male manager who yells only at female employees and not males may also exhibit discrimination if it is pervasive and directed at employees because of their sex.

Harassment does not only affect legally protected classes and can include, for example, offensive or derogatory remarks about a person's weight, hair color, or other physical attributes. There is no legal prohibition of teasing, joking, offhand comments, or isolated incidents. However, these actions can become harassment and illegal if the frequency or severity creates a hostile work environment or results in an employment decision that negatively impacts the employee. A harasser can be a co-worker, customer, client, the victim's supervisor, a supervisor in another area, and even a person charged with protecting the victim's rights, such as an executive, leader, or HR professional.

Diversity in the workplace is intended to express positive values and inclusiveness but can undesirably open a door for unprofessional, insensitive, or uninformed individuals to harass or discriminate against others. Unawareness of inappropriate behavior concerning someone's identity or diversity is a prime culprit for perpetuating a poor organizational culture and work environment. Harassment and discrimination are among some challenges that may surface within the culture. However, avoiding these pitfalls begins with educating all employees on the value of diversity, equity, and inclusion.

3.3 Unconscious Bias and Microaggressions

Most people are naturally wired to seek comfort in sameness. Examples are evident in human habits of repeated behavior like driving to work or going to the store. Individuals do things the same way because it becomes comfortable and familiar. When people are at work, at large events, or outings, they also tend to seek out behaviors, characteristics, or elements of the environment that may feel comfortable or familiar.

Behavior that becomes so routine that there is no longer a conscious effort to ensure it is proper can become ineffective and even dangerous. Consider an individual who has routinely walked one mile from a public transportation bus stop to his home each night after work. Habitually, the individual may have gotten accustomed to his surroundings and expectations of daily occurrences upon exiting the bus. Because he is often engaged in looking down at his phone and walking at a certain pace to make it home nightly, he may disregard an evident change that has occurred. Perhaps a violent perpetrator has followed him or noticed his inattention to his routine movements. A new circumstance that requires the man's deliberate attention now exists. The man's safety is put at risk if he fails to be aware of what he is doing, his surroundings, and anything that has changed. He must be conscious and diligent in his actions.

Although this example is far from a workplace scenario, it is indicative of something discussed earlier. Cultural, political, economic, and social climate changes affect what happens within individuals and at work. Those changes may or may not always be evident, drastic, or dangerous, but individuals must be diligent in their awareness. Awareness is what allows people, employers, and companies to adjust accordingly when the nature of what once felt familiar and steady has begun to shift.

Considering the many ways that individuals identify themselves and others, there are likely also many factors that influence a desire to seek sameness and familiarity, among others. Earlier, you learned that humans, even toddlers have a natural tendency to determine the relationship between things. Either people seek out similarities or opposites like a peg and a hole. Both desires are a normal human reaction, and both can result in finding comfort among peers.

Behaviors that attract the attention of individuals can become behaviors soon expressed by groups. The allure in establishing a relationship of sameness or unity is a natural inclination for individuals at work. There is something about group behaviors that pulls in others as the group grows and normalizes its actions. The organization's climate can subtly yet gradually change, and individuals must be diligent and aware as shifts emerge in the organizational culture.

An organization's culture has deeply embedded beliefs and values. They are perpetuated by the behaviors and actions of individuals within the company, even when those behaviors are not intentional. Biases and microaggressions are a part of organizational culture and reside at the deepest culture level. They should be explored and addressed to assess organizational culture effectively.

Biases

Sometimes individuals at work engage in deliberate actions intended to harm others. Certain situations may involve deliberate harassment or discrimination. However, sometimes discrimination may not be intentional, and the perpetrator may not even be aware it is occurring. **Bias** is also a behavioral act that can be a negative or positive attitude about a person or group but is more commonly viewed as a deliberate negative action against a person or others. However, biases can be implicit or unconscious, meaning there is a lack of awareness. **Unconscious biases (also referred to as implicit biases)** are often based on inaccurate or lack of sufficient information, causing a harmful impact on the workplace and its employees.

At work, executives may tend to communicate and hang out more with each other than they do with their staff. However, other factors may promote this behavior, such as the desire to maintain clear lines between reporting structures. IT and technical professionals may find a sense of comfort when working around other professionals with similar job functions. A group of Spanish-speaking people may gravitate toward each other over time and form a subculture within a particular department. These behavioral actions are examples of a specific type of unconscious bias commonly referred to as affinity bias. **Affinity bias** is where individuals have a tendency to gravitate toward people similar to themself. This bias can manifest in other ways like hiring or promoting someone who shares similarities in race, age, gender, or status. A hiring authority may express an unconscious bias or affinity for hiring someone and not realize that they have engaged in such an act.

A few other unconscious biases that commonly occur in a work environment include:

- **Attribution Bias** – Where a person tries to evaluate or understand why another person behaves the way they do

- **Beauty Bias** – Judging people based on perceived attractiveness and subsequently viewing and treating the person more favorably

- **Confirmation Bias** – A tendency to look for or favor information that confirms one's current beliefs

- **Conformity Bias** – When views are swayed or influenced by the views of others; similar to groupthink

- **Gender Bias** – To prefer one gender over another or assume that one gender is better for the job

- **The Halo/Horns Effect** – A tendency to think more highly of a person after learning something impressive or positive about them, or conversely, perceiving someone negatively after learning something unfavorable about them

- **Name Bias** – When someone judges a person based on their name and perceived background, often demonstrated when reviewing resumes or applications.

Microaggressions

The unspoken assumptions that occur within companies are a part of their culture. Although many actions are not predicated with words, they become consistent behaviors that result in culture among co-workers. Separate from biases, several factors can influence assumptions, behaviors, and workplace norms.

Some tangible examples include memos, employee handbooks, and other written correspondence promoting or perpetuating an idea or belief. While most work correspondence is intended to be a resource or positive tool for the company, some correspondence may not be professional. For example, some employees feel comfortable sharing jokes, emails, and texts in the workplace. Although this type of communication may be normal and acceptable in certain companies, the content can, and typically will, vary, and may be harassing, discriminatory, or even illegal.

When commonplace unspoken behavior or written correspondence negatively impacts a person or group because of the individual's or group's identity, microaggressions may be the culprit. **Microaggressions** are casual and frequent statements, actions, or incidents of indirect, subtle, intentional, or unintentional discrimination against members of a stigmatized or culturally marginalized group that occur in the form of slights and communicate hostile, derogatory, or negative attitudes.

Microaggressions veer beyond harassment and biases. They are categorized by insulting comments, statements, or actions hidden in the form of jokes and compliments that target and discriminate against a person's individual identity or group membership and subjects them to stereotypes. They are different from racism, sexism, and other forms of deliberate hostility because there is no harmful intent behind them. However, they are similar to biases in that the perpetrator is often unaware of the infliction of the comments or actions on others.

These aggressions may come from peers, co-workers, supervisors, or others. Workplace examples include statements like, "You're pretty for a black girl," "You're in better shape than I would think for an older man," or "You speak better than I thought you would even though you're from another country."

Although these types of statements may be intended as a compliment or attempt to say something positive, they are grounded in a slight discrimination against a person's identity. Microaggressions can also have adverse effects on an individual's health.

Reflection - Microaggressions

1. What are some ways that an employee handbook may express microaggressions?

2. What type of microaggressions might exist in emails, memos, or text messages?

3. How can organizations establish a safe and comfortable culture for their employees while also legitimately targeting specific buyers or audiences for certain products or services (ex: an all-male marketing team selling feminine hygiene products)?

4. Some people believe microaggressions are natural human behavior, and bringing them to the forefront allows oversensitivity to prevail in the workplace. Why is it essential to address microaggressions in the workplace from a perspective that does not assume or suggest oversensitivity?

Many marketing firms are tasked with targeting specific groups to sell products or services. Consider the following memo. What types of microaggressions may be felt by different individuals or groups? Which individuals or groups may feel directly targeted?

Figure 3.2

> **To:** All Staff at ABC, Inc.
> **From:** Janice, Chief Marketing Officer
> **Subject:** We did it!
>
> We are so excited to announce that our marketing team has finally penetrated the market on the south side of our city. As you know we have worked diligently for many months to procure business at BangUp Job Sporting Goods Supply Store. It has been a difficult but we were finally able to convince the community leaders in the area who are in favor of strict gun laws, to relax their notion that our client's Just4Me pistol would contribute to the black-on-black violence that was already rampant in the area. Of course, we all know that the product is not the issue, and we're excited that we were finally able to convince some of the community leaders to see how much this is a win-win for us all. Let's enjoy the new profits!
>
> Janice, Your Proud CMO

Remember that a work environment conducive to productivity has to be one in which individuals feel comfortable, safe, and valued. Therefore, microaggressions within the workplace are another way workers may feel out of place, attacked, or uncomfortable. Subsequently, these feelings can lead to health-related stress or other issues, anger, retaliation, depression, and can even lower work productivity and problem-solving abilities.

Even more detrimental, microaggressions also perpetuate stereotypes within the organization, moving from individualized targeting to a culture of shared beliefs about specific individuals or groups.

Avoiding Biases and Microaggressions

Microaggressions are vast and span different modalities like verbal and non-verbal infliction. They also affect diverse groups and individuals. Because microaggressions are imposed by individuals who typically are not aware of the act or words that are harmful to others, the first step to minimizing them is to increase awareness. Some tips for minimizing the occurrence of microaggressions and how to respond within a work environment include:

- Learn definitions and implications, so you are informed

- Increase awareness to recognize when microaggressions are inflicted, occurring, or imposed on others

- Understand and become aware of your own biases and microaggressions

- Develop and execute systems to prevent bias from interfering with hiring and workplace decision-making

- Seek diversity among peers, co-workers, employers, and others

- Practice active listening without defense. Allow others to express their sentiments.

- Do not be afraid of difficult conversations about identity, diversity, harassment, discrimination, biases, or microaggressions

- Promote a positive, diverse, and inclusive work culture free of bias and discrimination

- Demonstrate a receptive and calm attitude if others inform you of your microaggressions

3.4 Hiring Practices

Ideally, companies should attract, develop and retain a skilled workforce that contributes to the company's overall objectives. An organization's brand, culture, and commitment to diversity in the workplace are all tools that applicants and employees seek when considering potential employers. They are each a part of the organizational culture.

Employers of choice are companies that prevail when applicants, candidates, and employees are presented with alternative employment opportunities and options. A company's hiring practices are indicative of the organizational culture and demonstrate a commitment to attract talent based on skill and potential for roles. **Hiring practices** include the processes, procedures, and systems used to recruit, acquire, onboard, and train talent effectively. Poor hiring practices could lead to unqualified persons in positions and subsequently a decline in productivity and competitive advantage for the company.

Organizations typically work through a process moving from hiring to onboarding, where hiring includes sub-processes like talent acquisition, sourcing, screening, recruitment, and interviewing. Onboarding begins after an offer has been extended and an acceptance made by the offeree or a contract executed by all parties. After those preliminary processes, companies bring the individual onboard to begin work with the organization. The process may include orientation, training, or post-offer screening processes like background checks.

Hiring and onboarding processes can present some of the most challenging obstacles concerning diversity. The steps from hiring to onboarding are significant areas where many organizations fail to implement sound policies that are lawful, protective, and attractive to potential hires. Examples of practices, values, or policies that directly impact the successful hiring and onboarding process include:

- Poorly written job descriptions
- Lack of policies that acknowledge, embrace or nurture diversity within the workplace
- Lack of diversity on interview panels
- Biases in resume and application screening
- Pay equity issues (offering lesser pay for equal work to marginalized groups)
- Little to no training on diversity, equity, inclusion, ethics, legal hiring and interview practices, and other training for decision-makers
- Discriminatory or offensive cultural artifacts (statues, symbols, logos, etc.) held in high regard by the company
- Company brand perception
- Racist, sexist, homophobic, or other individual traits held by hiring managers and decision-makers
- Poor or stressed organizational culture

The result of poor hiring practices on the organizational culture can be detrimental. In turn, they affect company image, competitive advantage, and bottom-line profits negatively. To avoid these undesirable outcomes, organizations must identify and resolve diversity and equity issues to ensure the successful conveyance of their values.

3.4.1 Recruitment and Talent Acquisition

Talent acquisition is how human talent is acquired and added to a company's workforce. The process begins with identifying a need to fill a position. Companies determine where a gap lies between the need for an individual to perform a job and the potential output that would result from having the person perform successfully. Essentially, the human becomes the resource necessary to produce the output for the company. When employers seek out human resources to fill employment positions, it is referred to as **recruitment.** Subsequently, **selection** is when the company attempts to identify applicants or candidates with the requisite knowledge, skills, abilities, and characteristics to achieve the organizational goals. The company selects individuals to build its workforce and to fill position needs.

Selecting the best person for a job is often challenging. Multiple applicants with similar experience and qualifications can make it difficult to determine who is a better fit for the company. Hiring managers and decision-makers must understand the impact of putting the wrong people in the wrong positions. It is essential to identify where skills are needed and to assess talent properly so that recruitment and selection efforts are maximized based on reliable data. The key is to develop a sound job description to seek necessary skills, qualifications, and experience, but also to interview for an excellent organizational culture fit. Placing a skilled individual with proper credentials in a job is insufficient if the person does not share the company's cultural values to help grow and develop the company. A combination of clear and consistent processes and diverse and skilled interviewers to engage in the selection process is ideal.

Skills and qualifications required may vary from position to position. In some instances, companies may desire unique skills that directly impact their industry or organization. A CEO survey identifying areas in which employees lacked specific skills and how it adversely affected the organization is shown below:

Figure 3.3

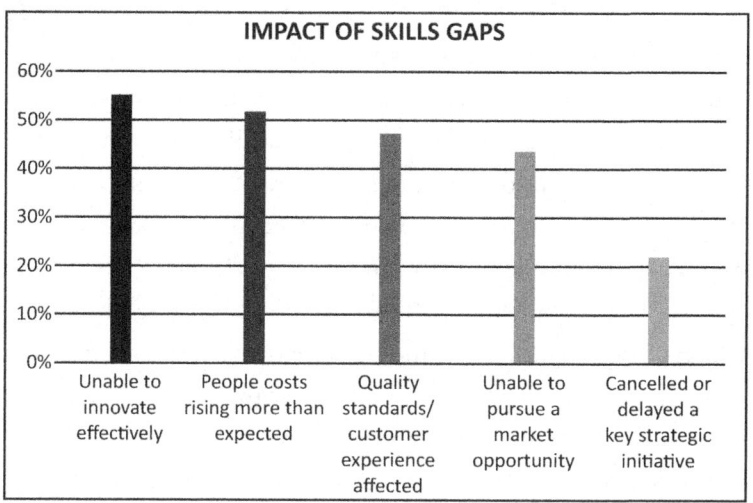

HR Magazine, vol. 65, no. 2, Summer 2020

Interview Panels

Interview panels are designed to help companies find and select the best talent. Multiple interview levels allow organizations to examine a candidate's potential for a position using various lenses. Several interviewers can help to ensure that a single person's perception does not round out the entire presentation an interviewee makes. In other words, one person may experience a halo/horns effect and not have an accurate assessment of a candidate's capabilities. Another may have some implicit biases. A third may not be as skilled or have the technical knowledge to assess the candidate's capabilities fully. Different interview levels and panel interviews provide an opportunity to eliminate certain biases that may otherwise affect the outcome of the recruitment and hiring process negatively.

Panels should minimally be diverse in race, gender, and status whenever possible. When panel representation is not diverse, it is both problematic and emblematic of several underlying issues. It may not always be possible to find diversity among panelists for every aspect of identity and diversity that a company attempts to protect or nurture. However, special efforts should be made to demonstrate a willingness to respect candidates who feel that diversity is critical in the interview and hiring process. Also, there is no guarantee that because an interviewee shares the same race, gender, age generation, or other characteristics with a panelist, the interviewee will feel satisfied with the process. The lack of satisfaction by some demonstrates the importance of intersectionality. The goal is not to satisfy the personal desires of the candidate related to the hiring process. It is, however, to ensure a consistent, fair, legal, and justifiable process that incorporates diversity among decision-makers.

Reflection

1. Consider what you know about race, gender, gender identity, disabilities, and other forms of diversity. What types of issues can happen if a job description includes discriminatory, offensive, or insensitive content?

2. What content examples may be considered offensive or inappropriate in a job description?

3. Which type of bias is most prevalent when screening resumes?

4. How could this bias negatively impact the hiring process?

5. Some companies have a structured interview process and multiple interview levels. What are some interview processes or practices that may adversely affect proper talent selection?

3.5 Bias in Artificial Intelligence (AI)

People, processes, and systems drive the workplace. This book has primarily focused on the diversity among people and policies and practices to promote an inclusive work environment. However, most organizations are also grounded in technology. Technological systems help implement the processes that are often devised to structure an organization. The human resource management function of most organizations is responsible for operating and maintaining the technology and systems that facilitate effective recruitment, onboarding, performance management, training, and other functional areas related to growth and development for the company.

Various systems that may be utilized within a company include Human Resource Management Systems (HRMS), Applicant Tracking Systems (ATS), Human Resource Information Systems (HRIS), Human Capital Management Systems (HCM), and Customer Relationship Management Systems (CRM). Technology in human resource management thrives on the abilities of the individuals managing the technological processes. However, some complex systems are designed to relieve human function to make processes more efficient, seamless, and effective for the company. The most effective systems integrate human skills and thoughts with other technological innovations.

Although the intent is to relive humans of tedious or difficult functions, incorporating technology can present human-machine conflicts. Where there is a discrepancy in the processes or decision-making and ethics, there has to be an overriding authority. Ensuring that no biases exist can be a complex task, but is not impossible.

Artificial Intelligence (AI) in the workplace refers to the combination of hardware and software like computers or computer-controlled machines that can simulate human intelligence in various ways. Examples of artificial intelligence include laptops, cellphones, robotics, and software programs. Each of these products or devices is designed to mimic and enhance human intelligence and capabilities.

HRMS database management makes it easy to store and retrieve data readily. Historically, this process was done manually for various areas of company operations and record keeping. With system integration, organizations can now manage specific tasks like leave of absence administration much better. Some software and systems can initiate a request and approval workflow and even disseminate responses indicating approval or denial. This type of integration is beneficial and time-saving. However, imagine that the system approves requests for some individuals and not others based on a factor that should not be considered. For example, an individual's race, ethnicity, or sex should not determine if a leave of absence request is approved or denied. If a circumstance exists where AI assesses and misinterprets data, there could be detrimental effects to the organization.

To build a solid and diverse workforce, a company's strategy should include non-bias talent acquisition, employee training, and retention of skilled workers. Incorporating technology into these organizational goals must be free from biases in artificial intelligence. AI can assess large amounts of data to devise information that humans can use to benefit the organization. For example, a job description for an entry-level cashier position may be posted through an Applicant Tracking System (ATS). The ATS can be programmed to search for keywords related to job experience. The system can filter out candidates whose information does not meet minimum qualifications, required years of experience, skills, or other desired attributes. However, imagine that the same system filters out candidates based on their sex or name. This type of filtering is undoubtedly undesirable and would indicate a bias in artificial intelligence.

Ethics, values, and beliefs are unique to humans versus technology. Technology does not establish or determine ethics. However, human ethics and values can be reflected in devices and software that humans program. Humans initially determine the outputs they desire and configure technology to produce them. Technology builds on patterns and algorithms to identify the likelihood of a human action and then attempts to mimic it. What could happen if a person's biases, discriminatory values, or beliefs are embedded in the system, even if done unknowingly or unintentionally?

Consider the example of software determining how leave of absence is administered. While the software can determine the number of days an individual has been absent from work, it cannot determine empathy, emotion, or extenuating circumstances. For example, a horrific incident where multiple employees are affected due to a natural disaster in a specific community may require additional leave of absence. AI that relies solely on algorithms and data may deny a request that should circumstantially be approved for extenuating reasons.

Some artificial intelligence vendors believe tools can help eliminate biases. Frida Polli, CEO of assessment provider Pymetrics, believes, "Metrics that are highly correlated with demographic identity are never going to be the best option for achieving fair outcomes. Unfortunately, much of the data that's used in conventional hiring processes, like standardized test scores and alma maters, has the potential to exacerbate historical patterns of inequality."

The following primary areas of technology and artificial intelligence should be examined to ensure that no biases, programs, or software exist to present issues with diversity, equity, or inclusion:

- Recruitment
- Payroll management
- Time Management
- Recruitment
- Employee Training and Development

- Records Management
- Performance Management
- Employee Compensation
- Systems Access for identical positions

Two prominent programming techniques used in artificial intelligence are natural language processing (NLP) and machine learning. NLP is a branch of AI that allows computers to comprehend text and spoken words the same way humans can (e.g., Alexa or Siri). Machine learning uses step-by-step patterns, data, and algorithms to mimic the way humans learn.

Some common current types of AI include:

- **Spam detection** - to scan e-mail and identify text patterns for routing to a junk folder
- **Machine translation** - to quickly translate e-mail, website content, presentations, and other documents into various languages to enhance internal communication
- **Sentiment analysis or opinion mining** - to analyze large amounts of text to determine if the data is positive, negative, or neutral (often used to online and social media content)
- **Text summarization** - to extract key information from original texts and create concise summaries
- **Robotics,** including delivery robots, security robots, recycling robots, AI-based drones, and others

Reflection

1. What are some areas where automation may present challenges or biases?

2. What are some pros and cons of automation that include human oversight or review?

3. What types of jobs or functions are less likely to be automated?

4. What types of human skills do these jobs involve?

Quiz

1. Kesha is typically the friendliest person in the office. She loves daily interaction with her co-workers and makes a habit of initiating small-talk with her peers. Josh prefers to refrain from small talk and one day responded to Kesha by saying, "You seem to have a lot more on your mind than I could have imagined just by looking at you." Josh's comments most closely demonstrate which of the following?

    a. Unconscious bias

    b. Discrimination

    c. Microaggression

    d. Harassment

2. What are the primary levels of company culture?

    a. Underlying Assumptions, Artifacts, Espoused Values

    b. Artifacts, Symbols, Policies

    c. Underlying Assumptions, Biases, Microaggressions

    d. Espoused Values, Symbols, Artifacts

    e. None of the Above

3. Which of the following are areas where a company's technology can present biases? Select all that apply.

    a. Performance Management

    b. Recruitment

    c. Anonymous Surveys

    d. Company-sponsored talent shows

4. Which word is best defined as the shared underlying assumptions, behaviors, and ways of interacting that contribute to an organization's environment?

   a. Cultural identity

   b. Organizational culture

   c. Reflection

   d. Diversity

   e. Underlying assumptions

5. Which of the following most accurately defines the Halo Effect?

   a. Treating a person more favorably based on their religion

   b. Gravitating toward persons similar to oneself

   c. Thinking more highly of a person after learning something positive about them

   d. Engaging in beauty bias

| **Answers** | 1 – c | 2 – a | 3 – a, b | 4 – b | 5 – c |

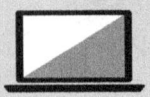 *Detailed Explanation to the above questions can be downloaded from the **Online Resources** section of this book on **www.vibrantpublishers.com***

Chapter Summary

- Organizational culture is the shared underlying assumptions, behaviors, beliefs, values, and ways of interacting that contribute to an organization's environment.

- Three levels determine how a culture manifests in a company: artifacts, espoused values, and underlying assumptions.

- Cultural identity varies for each company.

- An organization's values, artifacts, and underlying assumptions must align to create a strong organizational culture.

- Harassment is unwelcome behavior and can interfere with an employee's work performance.

- Discrimination against a protected class is illegal.

- An organization's culture has deeply embedded beliefs and values.

- Bias is a behavioral act that is seemingly a deliberate negative action against someone else.

- Unconscious biases are often based on inaccurate or lack of sufficient information causing a harmful impact on the workplace and its employees.

- Microaggressions are categorized by insulting comments, statements, or actions hidden in the form of jokes and compliments that target and discriminate against a person's individual identity or group membership and subjects them to stereotypes.

- Poor hiring practices could lead to unqualified persons in positions and subsequently a decline in productivity and competitive advantage for the company.

- It is essential to identify where skills are needed and to assess talent properly so that recruitment and selection efforts are maximized based on reliable data.

- Interview panels should minimally be diverse in race, gender, and status whenever possible.

- Artificial Intelligence (AI) in the workplace refers to the combination of hardware and software like computers or computer-controlled machines that can simulate human intelligence in various ways.

- Technology does not establish or determine ethics. However, human ethics and values can be reflected in devices and software that humans program.

Chapter 4

Equity

Chapter four unveils the idea of equity and how its construct is distinctly different from equality. These terms are used to demonstrate a central theme of fairness and justice and the different approaches that help achieve those results. This chapter incorporates survey data identifying groups or individuals within organizations who typically take on the DE&I leadership initiative. It further examines various types of equity and explains how inequity in a company impacts organizational health. The chapter relies on the comprehensive information about identity and diversity from previous chapters to expand the notion of diversity, equity, and inclusion. Chapter four incorporates reflection studies to enhance the reader's practical understanding and application of key concepts.

Primary learning objectives should include the reader's understanding of the following:

- Definition of key terms: equity, equality, employee engagement, job satisfaction, job satisfaction rate, compensation, affirmative action

- Understand various types of equity and their organizational impact
- Identify different individuals or groups that typically lead DE&I initiatives in organizations
- Differentiate the concept and construct of equity and equality
- Determine how pay equity and other equity issues can be addressed within a company

A 2021 survey report in the Fall edition of HR Magazine titled Diversity, Equity, and Inclusion Employer Trends revealed that DE&I (that is, diversity, equity, and inclusion) efforts could be initiated or led by several people within an organization. The survey indicated the organization's Chief HR Officer as at least partially responsible for DE&I efforts at 52% of the 383 U.S. employers that XpertHR surveyed in May 2021. If multiple people shared responsibility for the effort in the organization, respondents could choose more than one option. The survey further revealed that a CEO, president or owner accounted for 36%, and others, such as a board of directors, made up 19%.

About 17% of the companies in the survey reported that there was no designated person or group to lead their DE&I efforts, while 15% of the companies reported that volunteer employee groups contributed to their DE&I commitment.

Other survey results identifying company pioneers of DE&I efforts include:

- Chief DE&I officer - 11%
- Chief Operating Officer - 7%

- Chief Financial Officer - 5%
- General Counsel - 4%
- Outside Consultant - 2%

Traditionally, organizations measured their success and health primarily by their ability to produce bottom-line profits. If a company could engage in its core functions and have those operations result in profits and gains, then it was thought to be in good shape. The company's ability to effectively respond to changes in economic climates governed the organization's success. However, as the workforce and work environment were recognized as contributing factors to the bottom line, a stronger lens was used to examine a company's overall organizational health. Now, diversity, equity, and inclusion (DE&I) are vital components affecting the employees who ultimately impact a company's operations. Designated individuals like a Chief DE&I Officer or employee-led committees are tasked with creating programs and policies and fostering a culture that looks deeper to understand and nurture diversity, equity, and inclusion.

The deeper lens focuses more stringently on humans as the most valuable resource within any organization. It highlights the areas that negatively impact human or employee performance, behavior, satisfaction, engagement, and other inclinations affected by work and the work environment.

Different indicators help identify areas that directly affect how the company functions and people's perceptions about the company's health. Several departments within a company are tasked with aligning their departmental goals with their overall vision, mission, and objectives. To determine if departments are meeting their goals, many organizations utilize systems and processes that involve creating and tracking metrics associated with specific strategic goals.

Researchers, statisticians, and others have identified several metrics that determine organizational health. Some metrics include employee engagement, absenteeism, retention, job satisfaction rate, pay equity, and others. Ideally, when applied and evaluated correctly, the metrics identify areas that adversely affect the company or its employees. Specifically, recent efforts to unravel the benefits of diversity, equity, and inclusion, have presented opportunities for companies to realize their inconsistencies, inequalities, and ultimately inefficiencies.

The focus on closing the gaps identified by different metrics and results led to a deeper dive into reasons employees were not productive, engaged, or satisfied at work. For example, some employees are not attracted to the idea of giving or doing any more than what is required of them. The thought of participating in a department potluck or company softball team is off-putting. They also may lack motivation and engagement in their work. **Employee engagement** measures and examines how much employees care about their work relationships with leadership, co-workers, teams, company programs, and growth opportunities.

Consider a job satisfaction rate. **Job satisfaction** is the level of overall contentment an employee experiences concerning their job. The **job satisfaction rate** considers the total number of employees who report being satisfied divided by the total number of employees. It measures employees' satisfaction with the work itself. However, work and performance can be disrupted when employees are not content with the environment, pay, culture, or other factors affecting their work.

Disengaged employees are indicative of a bigger picture. When employees are not engaged, turnover, productivity, absenteeism, performance, and other pertinent areas of organizational health are affected. Generally, employees can be disengaged, lack motivation, experience dissatisfaction, and have performance issues if diversity, equity, and inclusion are not adequately addressed and nurtured from within the company. To build on the concept of diversity in the workplace, individuals and organizations must also examine equity in the workplace.

Equity refers to being just and fair toward individuals who have different circumstances and allocating specific resources and opportunities that each individual needs to reach equal outcomes. Equity relies on equality, justice, and fairness but is distinctly different in its original construct.

Many organizations have sought the progressive approach to valuing diversity by evaluating what is equitable within their organization and culture. It is critical to understand that although diversity may be embraced, fairness or equity may still be insufficient or non-existent. The two concepts are not mutually exclusive. Focusing on diversity and failing to examine equity can lead to increased problems rather than remedy issues.

4.1 Equity vs. Equality

Equity and equality are often confused or used interchangeably by individuals who are less familiar with their intent and construct. Although both terms refer to an idea of creating fairness, the two are distinctly different in approach. Both terms can refer to individuals or groups seeking the same outcomes related to fairness and justice.

Equity looks at individuals to determine what resources, assistance, or opportunities are needed specifically to align with others so that each person can reach equal outcomes regardless of circumstance. It relies on allocating different resources or opportunities rather than determining a fixed set of resources for everyone. Although the objective is to promote justice and fairness, equity is sometimes viewed by some individuals as unfair or discriminatory. On the surface, it may appear that while some people are given more things to establish equity, those people have a more significant advantage over the individuals who are not provided the exact same resources. However, the construct of equity refutes the notion that providing the exact same resources helps achieve equity.

Contrarily, **equality** focuses on providing everyone with the same things aiming to result in fairness and justice. It is often viewed as a measure of ultimate fairness. However, the concept of equality disregards circumstance and the premise that not everyone starts from the same place or needs the same things to achieve an equal result. Therefore, because situations and circumstances vary, merely offering the same thing to everyone will not likely produce the same outcomes for all.

Equity is consequently a revelation that does not seek to replace equality but to broaden the scope so that circumstance is considered when determining fairness. Paula Dressel from the Race Matters Institute stated, "The route to achieving equity will not be accomplished through treating everyone equally. It will be achieved by treating everyone justly according to their circumstances."

Figure 4.1

EQUALITY VS EQUITY

Equality and Equity Concept Illustration. Human Rights, Equal Opportunities and Respective Needs. Modern Design Vector Illustration By Anch – Adobe Stock File#: 410128567

Reflection

1. Consider what you know about identity and diversity. What are some circumstances that an individual or group of individuals may have that would prompt a push for equity within an organization?

2. Why might some individuals perceive equity as unfair?

3. What issues might a company experience when trying to ensure equity?

4. Recall what you learned about different learning styles (VARK). Equity suggests that because everyone does not learn the same way, learners may require different resources. What are some resources that different employees may require to assist with their learning needs

4.2 Types of Equity

At work, equity can be evaluated and demonstrated in different ways. It is often realized in pay equity, but equity constructs are also around training, power, race, ideas, conditions, and resources.

Training

Typically, companies provide some form of immediate training for their new hires. Organizations may devise elaborate or simple onboarding programs that include orientations, tours, or other processes to acclimate employees to the company. These processes may involve some type of training or transfer of information to groups in mass settings, assuming that all people need to know the same information. Sometimes the information is distributed individually, but the information is the same for each individual regardless of other circumstances like hire date, position, or department. Once an employee is fully integrated into the company, they may or may not receive additional training. Sometimes the training is referred to as on-the-job training (OJT). Other training may be designated for specific roles and focus on professional development opportunities only.

All company training should ultimately add to business value. When companies fail to recognize an immediate correlation between training and business value, the training is often cut or discontinued. However, business value should also consider and incorporate the skills and diversity among individuals to ensure equity where needed. For example, customer service and customer satisfaction training may be just as valuable as security awareness training, depending on the company. Some positions are more prone than others to violence, criminal activity, or incidents that may require extensive security awareness training.

Equity in training promotes the idea that some positions, companies, or cultures may require different training for some groups or individuals, and not all training is appropriate for all staff. For example, a bank teller holds a customer-facing position that may expose the employee to several interactions. They must have exceptional customer service skills and the training that aligns with those skills. However, it may be equally crucial for the teller to receive security awareness training. Such training would equip a teller with the knowledge and awareness necessary to recognize potential physical threats posed by seemingly typical customers. On the other hand, a remote-working account auditor for the same bank may not require either of those training resources.

Therefore, training equity should also evaluate individuals or groups based on circumstance. The decision to allocate training resources based on specific needs may prove more beneficial for organizations that would have otherwise required all employees to engage in generic training regardless of the role or function.

Work Flexibility

Before the COVID-19 pandemic, many organizations had either experimented with or partially utilized remote workforces. The concept of flexible work hours was not foreign, yet it varied based on the company, its operations, and often whether it was a global organization. Several companies understood the benefits of remote workforces and considered it an attractive recruitment tool to dangle in front of diverse and global talent. However, at the onset of the pandemic and months to follow, organizations soon realized that to maintain business as usual, they would have to explore more facets of work flexibility.

According to an article by Tam Harbert in the Fall 2020 edition of HR Magazine, "The Coronavirus pandemic not only expanded HR's corporate influence but also led to a renewed focus on employees."

Substantial financial losses in a short amount of time forced companies to shift into emergency mode. Subsequently, businesses had to figure out how to reengage employees, how to retain them, and how to leverage every aspect of what the employee could contribute to the company. The crisis led employers to rethink their previous convictions about working from home.

Previously, management and leaders within companies made decisions about working from home based on non-existent or non-comprehensive policies. A manager in one department might approve a work from home option for an employee, while a manager in a different department might deny the same request from a different employee with comparable circumstances. These types of issues demonstrated inconsistency and inequity in work flexibility.

Equity makes it critical to understand job roles, functions, and expectations before determining job flexibility. Consider diversity elements like status, gender, or job type. A facility janitor obviously cannot accomplish work functions working remotely. Therefore, the janitor's job role presents a unique circumstance different from someone with a different role. In this case, refusing to allow remote work based on job functions or role is legitimate and does not allow room for remote work consideration. However, well-crafted policies should clearly indicate that the company ensures equity in this area, yet exceptions are considered based on the ability to perform work duties from home.

Other diversity elements such as gender, race, or age do not permit a legitimate reason to distinguish remote work or flexibility options. Equity in work flexibility should be evaluated similarly to other equity types. Tracking metrics based on various factors, including diversity elements, should help identify equity issues in work flexibility.

Employees who are disengaged from the culture may experience equity issues with work flexibility. Even employees who are permitted to work from home may find that the policies do not support them or reflect changes that should be reevaluated. For example, dress codes, meeting attendance, and tardiness are common areas where employers have failed to update policies specific to remote workers.

Reviewing equity in these areas may unveil a need to alter meeting times, remote work resources, or other policies that directly impact some workers but not others.

Racial equity

Discussing race or racial issues within a company can feel quite uncomfortable for most people. The topic raises questions and awareness that many organizations may not be ready to face. Some organizations embrace the subject but are unable to convince employees that they should not fear the conversations. For employees, the topic may feel personal, and discussing racial equity could result in an expression of anger or other emotions that employees would rather not manifest.

Racial equity is a condition that can be achieved by the continual and intentional process of changing policies, practices, and systems to eliminate racial disparities and create positive change for marginalized groups who have experienced disadvantages and adversity based on color.

Consider what you know about identity and diversity. Reflect on individuals who have been disadvantaged based on their skin color, race, ethnicity, or gender. Workers with various types of diversity may have experienced difficult employment situations such as discrimination in hiring practices, promotions, or treatment within the company. Some discrimination, harassment, or other adverse treatment may have occurred for many years within a company without ever being addressed. For example, a U.S. company founded by Asian men may have started with all Asian workers. As the company continues to grow, the founders may gradually embrace racial diversity and hire other individuals. However, those workers may have been subjected to lesser pay for equal work in the same positions than their Asian counterparts who were hired on earlier. This type of discovery does not initially demonstrate racial discrimination. However, it raises awareness that there may be equity issues tied to race within the company culture. The more oppression or injustice is prolonged, the harder it will be for a company to recover, adjust and continue to grow.

The conversation around racial equity is problematic because it is difficult for companies to determine whether an entire race should be given additional tools and resources or if equity should focus on the individual. Just because a person shares the same race as others, it does not mean that all of their circumstances related to employment have been similar. Thus, the concern of whether equity should be based on race as a whole becomes a more complex dilemma.

Race-focused conversations can quickly disrupt seemingly harmonious environments. Many people may lack a thorough understanding of history, impact, terminology, and the awareness necessary to engage in constructive communication on the topic. However, several steps have been taken at various levels to bring awareness to inequities concerning race in companies. Over time, legal orders and policies have also been put in place to address racial equity issues.

Affirmative Action

Affirmative Action is a concept that appeared in President Kennedy's Executive Order 10925 in 1961. Its context included the allocation of resources or employment. The procedures were intended to eliminate unlawful discrimination against applicants, correct the effects of prior discrimination, and prevent future discrimination. A portion of the order read, "The contractor will take affirmative action to ensure that applicants are employed and that employees are treated during employment, without regard to their race, creed, color, or national origin."

In general, any employer who contracts with the government or who receives federal funds is required to document their affirmative action efforts, including metrics and practices. This book will discuss Affirmative Action, the Civil Rights Act of 1964, The Equal Employment Opportunity Commission (EEOC), and other legal remedies again later in the text under Laws vs. Practices.

Reflection – Training Equity

Think about training in a medium or large organization. Consider the concept of equity. What are some potential training equity issues that may exist between workers with different statuses or positions within a company?

4.3 Pay Equity and Compensation

Pay equity evaluates a company's compensation system to determine if it is fair and impartial and also identifies biases that take place when determining employee salaries. Pay equity may be difficult to quantify but should be tracked so that data can be reviewed and analyzed. Employees should always be compensated fairly. Different job roles are compensated differently, but the same or similar roles should be structured around a compensation system that identifies similarities in the functions of a position. Compensation should be justifiable based on job duties. However, it should also ensure that individuals with similar jobs are being paid equitably, regardless of qualities such as race, gender, or sexual orientation.

Companies can initiate pay equity by auditing salaries for the same positions and determining if biases exist without respect to increases for performance or other justifiable changes.

Equity is a partial solution for closing the gaps that have long existed between men and women and individuals whose race is associated with a marginalized group. One of the most prevalent pay equity issues in organizations is the pay variance female employees have received compared to their male counterparts in almost every industry. Similarly, Black or African-American individuals have traditionally earned less when compared to white people who hold the same positions. These types of disparities in pay reflect more deeply-rooted issues that can be unveiled and challenged through diversity appreciation.

According to the Spring 2021 edition of HR Magazine, "For every dollar that a white man makes, Black men make 88 cents, and Black women make 76 cents when comparing their median salaries. The gap reflects, in part, the types of jobs they hold. Nevertheless, even when the data is controlled for similar education and experience levels and similar geographic locations, Black men and women make less than white men."

Figure 4.2

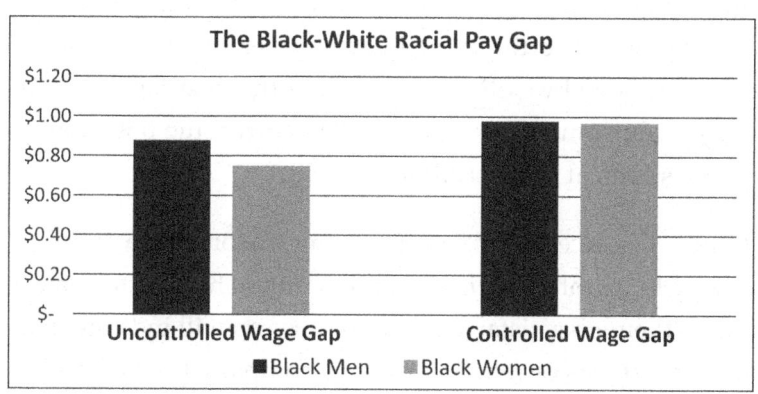

Source: PayScale.com, 2020 – Data from HR Magazine, Spring 2021 ed.

According to 2020 Bureau of Labor Statistics data, women are paid approximately 82.3 cents for every dollar a man earns. Additionally, women have traditionally received fewer growth opportunities that would potentially lead to increased pay.

Lawmakers continue to take on gender pay gaps that extend beyond equal pay for equal work laws by introducing legal bans that prevent employers from asking candidates about their salary histories. However, state and federal laws do not yet coincide, as various states prohibit employers from asking candidates about salary history, but federal law does not.

According to Jacqueline Cookerly Aguilera, a labor and employment partner with Morgan, Lewis & Bockius LLP in Los Angeles, "Relying on a candidate's prior salary in determining the individual's new salary may perpetuate the systemic undervaluing of work for women and women of color and, in turn, lead to more wage disparities.

Race and gender disparities are among the more prominent pay equity gaps concerning workers. However, some gaps exist for more justifiable reasons, like education, previous work history and licensing and certification. In cases where the reasons are not substantiated by skill, credentials or other justifiable factors, employers must make a valiant effort to correct the potential disparities even at the recruitment level.

Employees accept positions for many reasons. They work diligently to maintain their jobs and often tie their performance efforts to their job satisfaction. Often, surveys will indicate that people accept jobs or remain loyal to a company for various reasons. They may be location, job satisfaction, good working relationships, organizational culture, and other reasons. However, decades of research indicate that pay has traditionally been among the most significant motivators of employee performance. When pay is not satisfactory, employees are more likely than not to express discontentment. Because equity issues can directly impact pay, they can also cause additional problems with employee satisfaction, performance, and more.

Compensation

Generally, organizations make a valiant effort to compensate their employees based on what they believe is fair. The problem is that not all companies have mastered the art of what the big picture entails. According to Salary.com's 2020 Pay Practices and Compensation survey, approximately 56% of organizations lack a formal process to address pay equity. 70% of companies do not have an established salary structure to manage pay.

Compensation is not only monetary pay. It comes in many forms and may include non-monetary, indirect, and direct methods of pay. **Compensation** is what workers receive in return for their contribution to the work and organization.

Policies and other guidelines may exist within a company that outline how individuals are compensated. Types of compensation may include base pay like salary; incentives such as bonuses or commission; indirect pay like vacation or sick days; insurance plans like medical, dental, or vision benefits; retirement plans, such as 401K; employee services, like education assistance; and more.

Imagine that a company has examined its base pay for all employees to ensure equity. If the company also fails to review total compensation, including the other types of compensation, pay equity issues may still exist. Therefore, employers must continue scrutinizing compensation and pay policies to combat racial, gender, and other equity issues.

Employers will not always be aware of pay equity issues. Recall earlier what you learned about unconscious or implicit bias. Unconscious bias does not only exist between individuals but can occur by an organization or its leadership also. When the company is unaware that it has engaged in bias practices or policies, pay equity issues related to compensation can surface boldly.

Similar to other forms of inequities within a company, employers can initiate audits to identify gaps and subsequently take strides to address them appropriately. State and local governments have passed legislation focusing on pay equity that has resulted in several trends among employers. Some notable progress in states' efforts to address equity includes expanding equal pay laws beyond sex to include race and other protected classes. Also, several states and cities have made it unlawful for employers to ask job applicants about their salary history. Along with legal advancement, HR professionals and other experts suggest that among auditing and other efforts, companies should look through a DE&I lens to obtain an accurate picture of DE&I commitment related to pay.

4.4 Organizational Impact of Equity Issues

Increasing DE&I in organizations can create a competitive advantage. Integrating a culture of DE&I practices into all aspects of the organization requires a commitment, transparency, and a desire for continual progress. Equity issues in a company affect workers on various levels. They impact employees from hiring to termination. Worker morale, satisfaction, and performance are a few of the many areas that can be directly affected by different inequities in the work environment.

Long-term impacts on the employees can lead to poor performance and subsequently less engaged workers who deliberately decrease productivity. In turn, the organization suffers financially and in other ways. The company culture is compromised, and the public perception may fuel attacks against the attempt to build solid and viable workforces.

Different types of innovative software have been created to help HR teams and organizations track metrics that identify equity issues. The software typically requires data points like race, age, date of hire, and other factors that can be audited, quantified, or reviewed. Some areas in which equity challenges may be experienced and subsequently adversely impact the organization are:

- Recruitment and hiring practices and policies
- Compensation and pay policies
- Training and development
- Performance management consistency
- Employee relations, including employee satisfaction, morale, and engagement, and
- Promotions and succession

Quiz

1. What does DE&I typically stand for?

    a. Diversity, Ethics, and Identity

    b. Diversity, Equity, and Identity

    c. Diversity, Ethics, and Inclusion

    d. Diversity, Equity, and Inclusion

2. Which word is best described as providing everyone with the same things to achieve fairness and justice?

    a. Equity

    b. Ethics

    c. Equality

    d. Fair Treatment

    e. Efficiency

3. Chaise is a customer service representative at his company. His coworker, Brandon, is an administrative assistant. Chaise complained that the administrative assistants receive better treatment because they can work remotely. In general, what type of complaint has Chaise made?

    a. Equity in gender treatment

    b. Equity in work flexibility

    c. Equity in training

    d. Racial equity

4. **Which of the following areas can be impacted by inequity in the work environment? Select all that apply.**

   a. Job satisfaction

   b. Employee performance

   c. Employee morale

   d. All of the Above

   e. None of the Above

5. **True or False. If companies focus and make a sincere commitment to improving diversity in the workplace, there is no need to examine equity.**

   a. True

   b. False

| Answers | 1 – d | 2 – c | 3 – b | 4 – d | 5 – b |

*Detailed Explanation to the above questions can be downloaded from the **Online Resources** section of this book on www.vibrantpublishers.com*

Chapter Summary

- Equity and equality both refer to an idea of creating fairness, but are distinctly different in construct and approach.

- Equity looks to determine and allocate the resources that are needed specifically for each person or group to reach a fair outcome.

- Equality looks to provide the same resources to individuals or groups regardless of circumstances to reach a fair outcome.

- Equity constructs at work can exist around pay, training, power, race, ideas, resources, conditions, and other areas.

- Work flexibility can present equity issues if some individuals or groups are permitted to have more flexible working arrangements than others.

- Racial equity is a common equity issue in companies. It is an intentional process to eliminate racial disparities and create positive change.

- Affirmative action is a legal concept that was intended to eliminate unlawful discrimination against applicants and to prevent future discrimination.

- Pay equity looks at an organization's compensation system as a whole to determine if it is impartial.

- Compensation is not monetary pay only.

- ◆ Pay equity issues often exist between men and women, white people and people of other races.

- ◆ Companies experience adverse impacts in various areas due to equity issues, including impact in recruitment, hiring, compensation, training, performance management, employee engagement, employee satisfaction, promotions, and other areas.

This page is intentionally left blank

Chapter 5

Inclusion

Inclusion is the central focus for chapter five. The chapter examines how intentional inclusion, stereotypes, stigmas, allies, advocacy, and anti-discriminatory acts each affect organizational culture. It builds on the previously referenced concepts of identity, diversity, and equity to broaden the scope of how DE&I is best leveraged within the work environment. Some statistical data concerning how DE&I can affect bottom-line results along with a focus on interweaving intentional inclusion are presented. Chapter five reveals the difference between diversity and inclusion and offers a brief history on women and inclusion in the workplace. It also highlights how stereotypes are perpetuated throughout companies and the specific stigmas related to teens and health-related issues. The chapter incorporates reflection studies to enhance the reader's practical understanding and application of key concepts.

> Primary learning objectives should include the reader's understanding of the following:
>
> - Definition of key terms: inclusion, intentional inclusion, stereotype, stereotype threat, stigma, stigmatized, ally, advocate
> - Explain how individual perceptions about identity can create stereotypes
> - Identify three main types of stigmas
> - Determine common stigmas that are attached to individuals or groups within the workplace
> - Understand how non marginalized groups or individuals can contribute to DE&I efforts
> - Explain why inclusion is a necessary component of diversity programs

DE&I has become a widely accepted concept prompting a global response by employers to understand and embrace the responsibility of diversity, equity, and inclusion within the workplace. Diversity in the workplace is insufficient when it does not include the dual responsibility of inclusion. Having different opinions, races, backgrounds, and other identities within the work environment does not guarantee effectiveness. Diversity among individuals and groups should also enhance outcomes for individuals, teams, and the company. Valuing diversity is critical to forming a strong organizational culture. However, inclusion is necessary to sustain the culture. **Inclusion** is the act of taking in as part of a whole, an individual or group, into a group or structure, to integrate, involve, and engage the individual with the group dynamics. It moves beyond the numerical representation of identity and incorporates authentic and empowered participation for a true sense of belonging.

For employees and team members to feel valued, inclusivity must reach beyond the invitation to join or merely participate in a group. The effort requires a commitment to interacting with people, understanding diversity and equity, seeking awareness, and connecting with people in terms that are deeper than just a welcome. Creating and cultivating an inclusive environment and culture requires participation from leadership, individuals, and groups. Every voice and perception matters when crafting the employee experience. Failing to listen and learn from all voices and perspectives about diversity within the workplace is a definite path to missing the mark.

A 2021 survey by Eagle Hill Consulting Employee Experience, examined how employees' experiences affect customer service. Consider employees who feel disregarded, discriminated against, or intentionally excluded from teams, groups, or organizations. The impact moves beyond the individual to people outside of the company. Ultimately, the customers feel the brunt of the mistakes made within the organization's walls. According to the survey:

- 64% of 1,003 U.S. workers surveyed believe that employee experience directly impacts their ability to serve customers,
- 70% said their feelings about their day-to-day work experience – negative or positive, impacts their productivity, and
- 38% reported that their organization places a great deal of importance on employee experience and satisfaction.

Diversity vs. Inclusion

Some form of diversity among individuals and groups is inevitable. There are no mirror images between two individuals or groups that do not have at least one fundamental difference in make-up. Remember that diversity is everything about the human race that makes one individual or group different from another individual or group. Embracing diversity allows organizations to leverage more talent, skills, and knowledge without regard to physical or other differences that may result in biases. Inclusion, on the other hand, is a methodology that helps companies leverage diversity more effectively. Inclusion can be more strategic. It is a deliberate exertion that recognizes diversity first and also extends a welcome or demonstrates an open invitation to join, participate, or belong.

5.1 Intentional Inclusion

A company's commitment to inclusion must extend further than a process step in a DE&I program design. Cultures should minimally be safe and engaged. However, working to build strong and diverse cultures requires more extensive effort. Building inclusive work teams and environments help to strengthen cultures. **Intentional inclusion** is a deliberate effort to include people, ideas, or things that will enhance the overall knowledge, skills, performance, or other outcomes of a group, team, or environment.

Practicing inclusiveness involves recognizing various talents, skills, and qualifications within the workplace and allowing diverse talents to showcase their skills for the company's betterment.

Intentional inclusion also affects the company's bottom line. There are several advantages for companies that engage in inclusivity. Consider the various ways in which individuals, teams, or groups might be diverse. When an organization or group engages in intentional inclusion, it deliberately attempts to enhance its impact by valuing its members. Some companies actively seek people diverse in race, gender, veteran or military status, physically disabled, and other diversity identifiers. A data source in the Fall 2021 edition of HR Magazine reported that companies that actively sought people with disabilities to work in their organizations experienced 28% higher revenue, doubled net income, and realized 30% higher profit margins. The bottom-line results can partially be attributed to customers who felt a deeper connection with the company. According to Jim Sinocchi, "When people see a company that reflects themselves, they're more likely to purchase goods and services from that company."

Increasing profits and branding are not the primary reasons companies consider intentional inclusion. The objective is to strive for inclusivity to create and facilitate a better environment for employees. In doing so, companies may find that they recognize gains in other areas not intentionally targeted. The act is also a direct reflection of the company's commitment to its values, culture transformation, and natural succession. Extending opportunities, invitations, and membership into teams, groups, and companies also reveal a heightened sense of civility that is often shoved to the background. Biases, discrimination, and other behavioral offenses disregard civility and leave DE&I efforts exposed to potential pitfalls. Intentional inclusion is a proactive means to avoid those pitfalls.

Before the coronavirus pandemic, remote work arrangements were not as prominent as they soon became after the COVID-19 pandemic became widespread. Initially, employees who were required to work at an office or facility daily were subjected to their ability to travel to and from work. For example, if an employee did not own or access personal transportation, they may have relied on others or on public transportation. Nonetheless, they were expected to get to work using their own resources. Even in interviews, hiring managers would ask, "Do you have reliable transportation that will permit you to arrive at work on time and regularly?" Recruitment was therefore thwarted as companies may have limited their recruitment to individuals who lived in close geographic locations so that employees would not struggle with transportation or tardiness issues. A recent shift to remote work and flexible work arrangements have presented new opportunities for individuals who may have initially been disregarded based on their ability to travel quickly and efficiently. Remote work helped companies promote intentional inclusion for people who may have usually been turned away based on their ability to travel. A new and vibrant pool of workers who were not identified by their need or ability to travel became an option and opportunity for organizations worldwide.

Inclusion should be intentional so that employee perception and experience are valued—however, not only employee perception matters. Customers, applicants, stakeholders, and other individuals keep a keen eye on the way companies treat those around them. Every voice and perception will ultimately infuse into the organization's culture. The underlying assumptions are formed by individual perceptions as well as demonstrations of shared behaviors. Intentional inclusion expresses value in diversity and provides a welcoming environment for individuals, groups, and teams to feel a sense of belonging.

A Brief History of Women and Inclusion

As late as the first part of the 19th century, women were still excluded from many day-to-day professions. Teaching and writing were among the few occupations where women were not deliberately excluded. Women were discriminated against by specific organizations and also barred from attending medical colleges and other organizations that catered to men specifically.

For many years, women were also not privy to higher-paying professions due to their lack of comparative education. The exclusion from higher education, certain professions, memberships, and organizations has stained women with a less desirable status than their male counterparts.

The end of the 19th century and most of the 20th century is marked by women who received lesser pay than men who performed the same work or held the same positions. When the market shifted later in the 20th century, women gradually gained some leverage with educational opportunities, increased pay, and opportunities for inclusivity where there had previously been no invitation.

Reflection

1. What are some ways companies can engage in intentional inclusion?

2. What are some ways groups or teams within a company can engage in intentional inclusion?

3. What types of teams, groups, or programs may exist within a company that lack inclusivity?

5.2 Stereotypes and Stigmas

A **stereotype** is a fixed idea or construct shared by many people about an individual, group, or thing that may be untrue or partly true. Individuals perpetuate stereotypes through words, perceptions, stories, and other means of reinforcing an idea. Correspondingly, prejudice is an attitude about another person or group based on stereotypes. Many researchers and scientists have conducted different studies about how stereotypes impact self-perception and the perception of others. The effects of stereotyping can be detrimental to any culture. In the work environment, stereotypes are prominent in signs (e.g., restroom signs), in job ads, memos, written performance reviews, training programs, and other company outputs. Written content and verbal expression within the workplace can reinforce stereotypes about race, gender, religion, national origin, age or other status characteristics, creating organizational culture damage and disadvantages for employees.

Stereotypes are promoted throughout organizations when written content or verbal expression targets cultures, groups based on particular shared identities, behaviors, and other factors.

Companies must be diligent in producing outputs that do not generalize groups of people in a manner that disadvantages them or subjects them to underlying perceptions. Organizations can address stereotypes promoted with the culture by reviewing emails, memos, documents, job ads, performance reviews, and other areas where generalizations may perpetuate an underlying idea about a group.

Individual perceptions about identity also create stereotypes. **Stereotype threat** is a concept that imposes a negative perception of self-characteristics regarding one's identity with a group. For example, a stereotype may exist that a woman cannot perform firefighter duties as well as a man. Although there is no evidence to support the stereotype, a woman's awareness of the notion can cause negative perceptions of her identity with a particular sex or gender. Subsequently, a female firefighter may question her ability, skills, or other characteristics that support her confidence regarding the occupation. The uncertainty can cause cognitive resources to be utilized to create a self-fulfilling prophecy.

Stigmas about identity and diversity are often introduced as a framework negatively impacting individuals and groups. A **stigma** can be defined as a mark of infamy or disgrace. Something or someone that is **stigmatized** is subject to a stigma or marked as an outcast. There are many stigmatized persons, groups, and things within society. They can range from groups like street gangs to a brand for a product like cigarettes. Both have historically been attached to a negative connotation, image, or representation that causes them to be perceived in a manner that works against their whole identity in one form or another.

The work environment is a microcosm of society. A company's culture varies just as much as the individuals and groups within them. Each element of diversity within an individual or group may entice others who feel comfortable observing, commenting about, or categorizing whatever they deem necessary. Specific elements of diversity have prompted stigmas, labels, and stereotypes that are not factually supported.

Erving Goffman is an American sociologist who identified the social theory of stigmas and introduced the term into theoretical constructs. Goffman considered stigmas as a means of spoiling identity and affecting a person's conformity to social norms. Thus, working against those elements an individual may hold in high regard personally or by persons around them.

According to Goffman, the three main types of stigmas include (1) stigma associated with mental illness, (2) stigma associated with physical deformation, and (3) stigma attached to identification with a particular race, ethnicity, religion, ideology, or another element of diversity.

A few common stigmas within the workplace are attached to the following:

- Individuals with mental health or health-related issues
- Teens
- Employees with disabilities
- Older workers
- Females in leadership roles
- White males

Figure 5.1

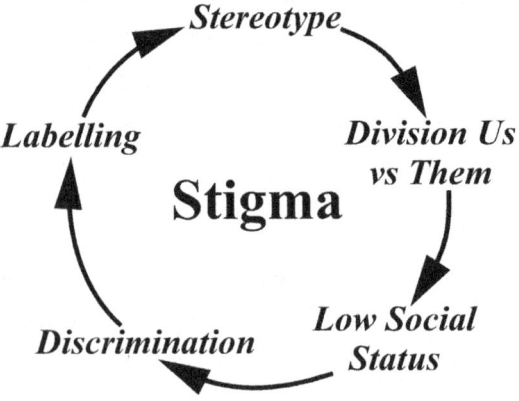

Components of Cycle of Stigma - Adobe Stock File #319538714

Ideally, training on identity, diversity, and inclusion should push employees to refrain from stigmatizing. However, stigmas are often deeply embedded in individual beliefs and experiences. The conversation around stigmas is vital to help transform cultures into environments that embrace and value diversity. The conversations should begin with civility and move toward a deeper understanding of stigmatization impact.

Teens

Although employers understand the value that younger workers can bring to an organization, teen workers are often stigmatized. Companies realize innovativeness, efficiencies, and other gains related to hiring younger, less experienced employees. However, a hint of hesitation looms in the background for many companies that hire teens. An article in HR Magazine, Summer 2020 edition titled "Teens are more vulnerable to workplace Hazards" references issues that may arise when working with teen employees. The article states, "Issues that may arise with hiring teens range from lack of experience, improper training, and lack of commitment for various reasons (like other priorities). However, these are all assumptions that a hiring manager may make to generalize a potentially otherwise exceptional hire." This type of generalization targets teen workers and quickly stigmatizes teens as a group. Subsequent acts related to inclusion, hiring, or training are all affected by stigmas that should be disregarded to avoid poor business decisions. Hiring decisions and biases such as these that would prevent hiring managers from extending opportunities for employees of various ages should be monitored carefully and taken into consideration to avoid legal issues and organizational culture demise. Intentional inclusion related to teen hiring with no age restriction for performing the job can be explored to address issues with teens and stigmas.

Health-Related Stigmas

The COVID-19 pandemic prompted a shift in work environments that led to immediate concerns for individuals working within companies, groups, or even close proximity to other employees. Political, legal, and social climates penetrated the office space and ignited emotions throughout many organizations.

As social unrest erupted, employers faced decisions that were not well-defined in the confines of an employee handbook or pre-written safety policies. Businesses had to make decisions related to their company operations that, for the first time, were directly affected by employees' health. Companies had to figure out how to address issues like mandatory vaccinations, refusal to be vaccinated, illness at work policies, social distancing, and more.

The coronavirus pandemic sparked stigmas about people who were vaccinated, not vaccinated, coughed at work, and even about those who may have been ill for other reasons. The emerging issues took a jab at general civility and other socially responsible behaviors. The stigmas about health-related illnesses at work fostered climates where underlying values and assumptions increased tensions throughout organizations. The national and global impact forced many companies to integrate diversity and inclusion training into annual curricula and adopt modified policies to address various issues tied to stigmas.

5.3 Allies, Advocacy, and Anti-Discriminatory Acts

As organizations encounter climate changes within and around them, they have begun to fortify their operations by embracing awareness, innovation, adaptability, and flexibility. These strategies have allowed companies to meet rapidly growing challenges and advance more quickly. However, swift changes within a company that are not well structured can also present difficulty for individuals, teams, and groups who have to adjust. It is imperative that organizational leaders, human resource teams, managers, and others lead the way so that employees are not lost in rapidly moving shuffles to meet demands or trials.

Intolerance plagues the work environment. An unyielding unwillingness to listen to why employees are discontent at work or even afraid at times is a challenge. Companies realize now, more than ever, that failure to listen and address issues like diversity and inclusion will result in much more impactful consequences.

Many forward-thinking companies have devoted time and energy to building strong Diversity, Equity, and Inclusion (DE&I) programs. Top-down leadership is an essential part of forming a progressive culture. Without the support, buy-in, and commitment from leaders, diversity efforts tend to dwindle over time. When leadership commits to providing training, support, open communication, and programs related to diversity, they are demonstrating advocacy for diversity and anti-discrimination. Employees are often equally committed to building diverse and vibrant cultures. Individuals often have a vested interest in ensuring their voices are heard and their needs

www.vibrantpublishers.com

met at work. Employees may choose to initiate a program, serve on a committee, or support DE&I throughout the organization in other ways. Whatever manner individuals contribute, their efforts are often to serve as an ally, advocate, or conduit for anti-discriminatory acts.

When diversity and inclusion programs are incorporated into business operations, employees may begin to ask how they can serve as an ally. They may wonder what they can contribute individually to build the culture they want to develop. There are several ways that individuals can aid in promoting diversity and inclusion. There are also many opportunities for organizations to establish inclusive programs that invite diverse opinions, perceptions, and experiences to the table. Training helps companies and employees identify ways to support and contribute to diversity and inclusion. It provides evidence that company leadership is not simply implementing a program and then turning their heads to ignore the deeper sentiments and desires of the workgroups and individuals.

Not all individuals who support DE&I programs and efforts are members of marginalized groups. Traditionally, those groups are identified by race, gender, sex, ethnicity, or religion. Persons not categorized by the traditional definition of a marginalized group may also support and believe strongly in diversity, equity, and inclusion within the workplace. Mary Abbajay states, "An **ally** is someone who is not a member of a marginalized group but who supports inclusion through stated values and positive action for everyone's benefit."

Kathy Gurchiek's article in HR Magazine (Spring 2021) on Influencing DE&I Strategies quotes Abbajay's suggestions for ways HR professionals can serve as an ally for an organization. Some steps include:

- Champion and amplify the ideas of other people by actively seeking their contributions during meetings and making sure ideas from a diverse group of colleagues are heard and supported

- Perform small acts of inclusion. When working or starting a project, for example, ask yourself how it can be made more inclusive, who has not been invited to a meeting, and how could the project benefit from other points of view

- Make an effort to get to know all your colleagues professionally and personally. Making friends at work sends a powerful message to others about inclusion and status

Creating an environment where employees are seen, heard, and respected for their personal and individual values is just as important as being respected for the skills and talents they contribute to their work. Allies, advocates, and accomplices work collaboratively to create positive change that will benefit a company and its diversity and inclusion work. An accomplice is someone who supports the target of oppression when they are going out on a limb.

Gradual changes within a company to form a more diverse culture helps to eliminate the unrest from harsh realities about discriminatory acts in the workplace. There is even more victimization when employees are criticized for expressing how they feel about not being heard, respected, or treated fairly by their employer. The employees' expressions are often subsequently communicated through social media, causing increased exposure to the company's failed attempts to protect and support its workers. Becoming an ally or advocate for diversity, inclusion, or anti-discriminatory acts is ideal for companies to avoid such exposure. It is also a way that individuals who feel they do not have a voice or place in the diversity and inclusion conversation can assert their interest and desire to help.

Fostering civility and building a culture full of allies and advocates requires creating trust between employers and employees. However, it also allows other individuals to experience authenticity and dedicate their efforts to the endeavors happening within the company.

Quiz

1. True or False. Extending an invitation to employees to join or participate in a group is generally a sufficient act of inclusion.

   a. True

   b. False

2. Which is a reason companies engage in intentional inclusion?

   a. To increase profits

   b. To decrease brand awareness

   c. To mask company commitment to organizational culture development

   d. To promote individuality

3. Which of the following is not a primary type of stigma presented in the text?

   a. Mental illness

   b. Physical deformation

   c. Racial diversity

   d. Human civility

4. Of the following, what type of result did the COVID-19 pandemic most likely cause for several organizations?

   a. Health-related stigmas

   b. Inclusion issues

   c. Diversity issues

   d. A decrease in anti-discriminatory advocacy

5. Which of the following is not a component of the stigma cycle?

   a. Discrimination

   b. Stereotype

   c. Labeling

   d. Inclusion

   e. None of the Above

| Answers | 1 – b | 2 – a | 3 – d | 4 – a | 5 – d |

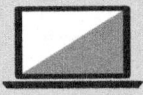

*Detailed Explanation to the above questions can be downloaded from the **Online Resources** section of this book on **www.vibrantpublishers.com***

Chapter Summary

- Diversity in the workplace is insufficient when it does not include the dual responsibility of inclusion.

- Inclusion is the act of taking in as part of a whole, an individual or group into a group or structure to integrate, involve, and engage the individual with the group dynamics.

- Embracing diversity allows organizations to leverage more talent, skills, and knowledge without regard to physical or other differences that may result in biases.

- Intentional inclusion is a deliberate effort to include people, ideas, or things that will enhance the overall knowledge, skills, performance or other outcomes of a group, team or environment.

- Stereotypes are promoted throughout organizations when written content or verbal expression targets cultures, groups based on certain shared identities, behaviors, and other factors.

- A stereotype is a fixed idea or construct shared by many people about an individual, group, or thing that may be untrue or partly true.

- A stigma is a mark of infamy or disgrace. Something or someone that is stigmatized is subject to a stigma or marked as an outcast.

- Three main types of stigmas include (1) stigma associated with mental illness, (2) stigma associated with physical deformation, and (3) stigma attached to identification with a particular race, ethnicity, religion, ideology, or another element of diversity.

- Diversity efforts tend to dwindle over time when there is no buy-in, commitment or support from organization leaders.

- Not all individuals who support DE&I programs and efforts are members of marginalized groups.

- An ally is someone who is not a member of a marginalized group but who supports inclusion through stated values and positive action for everyone's benefit.

- Allies and advocates work collaboratively to create positive change that will benefit a company and its diversity and inclusion work.

Chapter 6

Enhanced Diversity Literacy

Chapter six revisits some terms and definitions presented in earlier chapters. It expounds on diversity literacy and introduces new terms, concepts, and constructs. The chapter focuses specifically on race and various derivatives of the term, including racial privilege, racism, institutional racism, and more. It also focuses on age, religion, disabilities, and gender. Gender is examined in-depth to include a deeper concentration on gender identity, gender expression, and presentation. Chapter six incorporates reflection studies to enhance the reader's practical understanding and application of critical concepts.

Primary learning objectives should include the reader's understanding of the following:

- Definition of key terms related to gender identity and gender expression
- An enhanced understanding of how race, age, gender, religion, and disabilities are perceived in the workplace

- Identify various types of religions
- Explain the acronym or abbreviation: LGBTQIA+
- Identify and define various terms related to gender identity and expression
- Explain the purpose and impact of the Americans with Disabilities Act (1990)

Identity, diversity, equity, and inclusion are comprehensive ideologies that comprise several terms and definitions. The concept of each idea creates a funnel for deeper understanding, awareness, and knowledge about identity. Diversity literacy can be complex as people continue to expound diversity in identity. The workplace focuses on specific terms and identifiers to ensure legal compliance, social responsibility, cultural awareness, and other aspects of building vibrant teams and cultures. This text explores a few more commonly referenced terms within the work environment and provides a general overview of their meaning and impact. For a more in-depth review of some of the terms, readers can refer to Chapter 2.

6.1 Race

Chapter two revealed that race is central to identity and diversity and is also based on classifications of individuals who share distinct anatomical or physical characteristics, like skin color. More specifically, race is a socially constructed system of categorizing humans based mainly on observable physical features like skin color and ancestry. There is no certainty that race is a biological construct.

Certain legal entities have identified various races and assigned meanings that reference the origins of individuals associated with their race. However, race is not conclusive or absolute because individuals can choose to self-identify with multiple races or may not know their origin well enough to suggest a race. The general population who are not concerned with scientific or exact meanings often associate race with skin color. There are also social constructs about perceived race that help define the term in a non-biological way.

Race is also an ideology that has historically been used as a basis for domination, bias, and discrimination. It still has a prominent and lingering influence on social climates, identity formation, and self-perception, including behaviors and perceptions in the workplace. One's sense of self-esteem and value is often linked to aspects of their identity. Beauty, authority, belonging, status, and many other descriptive attributes can be associated with how people perceive their race. Social responses within specific cultures may dictate how a person's race is perceived. Actions like making positive comments about one's attractiveness, offering increased job opportunities, and other reaffirming gestures, signify how some people perceive race.

An experiment conducted multiple times, including in the 1960s, 90's, and other decades, documented the responses of young African-American girls. The elementary-school-aged children were seated in a room with a table that had one black doll and one white doll on it. Each girl was instructed to show their response by indicating which doll represented the best answer to specific questions. The questions were similar to, "Which baby doll is the good one," and "Which doll is the bad one." When the girls were asked about the good doll, the overwhelming response was each girl pointing to or identifying the white doll as the good one and the black doll as the bad one. The responses were deemed indicative of the perceptions the young girls had about their race. Stigmas, stereotypes, and an element of racial identity had been presumably imposed and subsequently internalized by the girls. When similar studies were conducted involving children of other races, including white girls and boys, the results were strikingly similar. The children primarily identified the white doll as good and the black doll as bad. If these notions existed and still exist among small children, it is likely that the cultural and societal perpetuation of such stereotypes and stigmas also make their way to the workplace.

Some terms derived from the core concept of race that affect workplaces and society include:

- **Racial privilege** – describes race-based advantages and preferential treatment based on skin color

- **Racial oppression** – refers to race-based disadvantages, discrimination, and exploitation based on skin color

- **Racial justice** – the systematic fair treatment of people of all races that results in equitable opportunities and outcomes for everyone

- **Racism** – a complex system of racial hierarchies and inequities. The individual or micro-level of racism is characterized by internalized and interpersonal racism. The broader level of racism extends beyond individual constructs and includes institutional and structural racism

- **Internalized racism** – describes the personal, racial beliefs of individuals that are created when people absorb social messages about race and adopt them as personal beliefs, biases, and prejudices

- **Internalized oppression** – (For people of color) can involve believing in negative messages about oneself or one's racial group. For white people, *internalized privilege* can involve feeling a sense of superiority and entitlement or holding negative beliefs about people of color

- **Interpersonal racism** – how people publicly intentionally, visibly, and verbally convey private beliefs about race when they interact with others; some acts may be a result of unconscious bias or take the form of bigotry, hate speech, or racial violence

- **Institutional racism** – refers to racial inequity within institutions and systems of power, such as places of employment, government agencies, and social services. It can take the form of unfair policies and practices, discriminatory treatment, and inequitable opportunities and outcomes

6.2 Age

Age is a component of diversity and identity. **Age** is the length of time a person or thing has lived or been in existence. There is, therefore, a scientific, biological, or numerical foundation that helps to determine an individual's age in many cases. However, in specific environments, the discussion about age can be relative. If a person states, "He is too old for the job," then the reference compares the individual's age to a requirement, desire, or belief of what the person's age should be to fulfill the job. If someone states, "She is younger than I thought," then the reference is comparing the individual to the person's perception of the age of another.

Some specific rules and laws pertain to age and hiring practices. It can be illegal to hire individuals of a certain age for specific jobs if they are not considered an adult. It can also be illegal not to hire individuals of a certain age if the decision not to hire them is based on their age rather than other factors determining suitability.

6.3 Religion

Religion is a social-cultural system of beliefs, faith, practices, and worship of a controlling power, especially a personal God or gods. Organizations are made up of individuals who have diverse backgrounds, including their religious and spiritual affiliations. Employees who have various religions are prominent throughout most workplaces. Companies that do not understand or value the personal differences in religion may find it challenging to create diverse, inclusive, and progressive cultures.

There are hundreds of religions worldwide. It is impossible to categorize individuals by religion, as it can also be fluid. Religion, faith, and beliefs can change over time. Some individuals may also practice multiple religions, creating a new element of diversity, unlike traditional religious constructs. Below are some traditional and common symbols associated with various religious constructs.

Figure 6.1

World religion symbols. Eight signs of major religious groups and religions. Christianity, Islam, Hinduism, Buddhism, Taoism, Shinto, Sikhism, and Judaism, with English labeling. Illustration. Vector. By Peter Hermes Furian Adobe Stock File #132028947

6.4 Gender

Remember that a person's **sex** is usually categorized as male or female and most often based on specific biological features like reproductive organs, hormones, genes, and chromosomes. Gender, however, refers to how a person identifies internally and expresses themselves externally. The work environment has presented challenges related to policies concerning gender. Company dress codes are perhaps the most prominent area where organizations struggle to craft uniform policies that are enforceable for multiple genders. Gender stereotypes lead to company content and output being subject to ridicule and criticism for their lack of consistency, accuracy, and fairness.

Examples of typical and evident disparities in company policies may include:

- Approval for women to wear open-toe shoes, but not approved for men
- Approval for women to wear skirts or dresses, but not approved for men
- Approval for women to wear long hair or ponytails, but not approved for men

Historically, women have had to overcome more discriminatory practices, acts, and ideologies associated with the workplace than men. However, as time progressed, additional oppressions and disparities concerning other marginalized groups have also become prominent. Gender identity and expression have presented enlightening perspectives that require companies to reevaluate policies and their historical correlations between a person's identity, sex, gender, and work requirements.

6.4.1 Gender Identity and Expression

A person's gender identity is how they identify themselves. Even at birth, sex is assigned. However, most people are not knowledgeable enough to ask about their chromosomes, sex, genes, and other biological traits as soon as they are born. They learn and embrace an identity over time. Typically, the identity is determined by whatever construct the person's immediate social and familial environment has formed for them. As time passes, a person's expression, opinion, or sentiment can change because gender identity is not always the same as one's biological sex or sex assignment at birth.

Gender identity is broad and permits a spectrum of identifying characteristics. Individuals may identify more personally with masculinity, femininity, multiple genders, or none at all. Internal feelings, external influence, upbringing, and many other factors can change or form gender identity. It is the essence of who a person ultimately believes and knows themself to be.

Reflection

A person wearing a dress, high-heeled shoes, nail polish, lipstick, and long hair may enter a restroom designated for women only. The person has traditional male features like a beard, a masculine/muscular physique, no breasts, and larger hands, typically associated with the male sex. A woman who is also an employee in the restroom sees the individual and assumes the individual's gender is male. She speaks to the individual and notices that the person's voice has a deep, raspy, and low tone. The woman rushes from the restroom and reports to security that a man dressed as a woman has entered the women's facility. She asks that he be removed immediately and suggests that he may be in the restroom to harm women physically.

1. What type of challenges could this scenario present in a work environment?

2. What if the woman in the restroom and the individual entering the restroom were both employees? Could this have prompted a different initial response by the woman who was already in the restroom? Why or why not?

3. Who is the best person to address this situation, where the woman believes she may be in physical danger?

4. If the woman does not feel she is in physical danger, what may be a good course of action for her to express her concerns?

5. What may be a good course of action for the individual entering the restroom to express their concerns, if any?

6. Why is gender identity important in this scenario?

7. What are some ways companies can begin addressing gender identity situations in the workplace?

6.4.2 LGBTQIA+

Gender identity, expression, and presentation are fluid. The terms address how a person views themselves, but also how they want others to view them. **Gender expression and presentation** involve mannerisms, clothing choices, name selection, pronoun choices, and other outward ways a person chooses to express or present themselves. The gender identity spectrum includes LGBTQIA+ and other identities. Individuals who identify with the spectrum work in various industries, professions, and locations. Globally, it is likely that many companies have diversity within them that includes gender diversity beyond binary sex identity. Organizations should be knowledgeable of different identities and expressions to ensure inclusive, diverse, and anti-discriminatory cultures.

Some self-proclaimed gender identities and definitions include:

- **Agender (neutral gender; null-gender; genderless; neutrois)** – A person who does not identify with any particular gender or that has no gender at all
- **Androgyne** – A person who identifies as a combination of masculine and feminine or on a scale between masculine and feminine

- **Bigender** – A person who identifies as having two genders

- **Butch** – A term typically expressed by women who identify as lesbians to describe the way they express their perceptions of masculinity; also considered a separate gender identity by some

- **Cisgender** – A person who identifies with the sex that they were assigned at birth

- **Genderfluid** – A person who has a gender identity and presentation that shifts between or shifts outside of society's expectations of gender

- **Gender-nonconforming** – People who do not conform to the traditional expectations of gender or whose gender expression does not fit neatly into a category

- **LGBTQIA+** – An abbreviation for the following: lesbian, gay, bisexual, transgender, queer, intersex, and asexual. The acronym is widely used to identify individuals who identify on the spectrum with various gender identities. The plus symbol is used to represent other sexual identities

- **Nonbinary** – A person who does not experience gender within the gender binary; identifiers may also experience overlap with different gender expressions, such as being gender non-conforming

- **Omnigender** – A person who experiences and possesses all genders

- **Polygender (Pangender)** – People who experience and display parts of multiple genders

- **Transgender** – A term that encompasses all people who experience and identify with a different gender than that of their assigned sex at birth. Identifying as transgender does not imply sexual orientation. Like cisgender people, transgender individuals can be straight, gay, bisexual, or of any sexual orientation.

- **Transitioning/Gender Transition** – A process that some, but not all, transgender individuals undergo to match their gender identity more closely with their outward appearance. This may include making changes to clothing, names, or pronouns, as well as addressing health care needs such as taking hormones or undergoing surgeries.

Historical Significance of "Coming Out"

Before the acronym and use of LGBTQIA+ was used to identify a community or culture, there was a considerable existence of individuals who engaged in gender identity and expression. Sexual orientation has long been a significant part of individuals' identity. However, from the 1930's to the 1950's, a growing backlash against people who identified as gay became increasingly prevalent. The initial response for many individuals was to live and act in secrecy concerning sexual orientation, gender, or gender identity. Due to the secretive lifestyle that many had begun living, "coming out" became a tormenting fear that was fueled by the hatred, ignorance, harassment, and other offensive behaviors of others. For example, in 1969, a group of patrons fought back against law enforcement officers who had raided a bar that at the time which was well-known for its gay or homosexual clientele. The stance against the officers took the form of riots and rebellion. Later, becoming known as the Stonewall Rebellion, the patrons' resistance was celebrated annually in what is known today as a march for "gay pride."

The marches and celebrations elicited sentiments that became associated with a desire to no longer be "in the closet." The term referenced individuals who were still living in secrecy to hide their sexual orientation. Contrastingly, other terms began to surface to address not living "in the closet" and were likened to the notion of "coming out."

However, even though some progress, awareness, and realization had been made through gay pride marches and other celebratory events, there was still a fear of what "coming out" would mean for individuals who were not yet ready to face the ridicule, self-hatred, hatred from others, harassment and misconceptions from society at large.

Today, some progress in education, awareness, and diversity appreciation has helped to dismantle fears that were once considered an insurmountable feat. Younger generations have had the opportunity to experience support, education, and awareness in areas concerning sexual orientation, gender identity, and expression that some older generations did not. As a result, younger generations are more inclined to identify with the LGBTQ community openly, moving away from the inclination to remain secretive about one's identity.

A Gallup poll conducted in 2020 revealed that more members of Generation Z identify as LGBTQ than members of older generations. Partially consequently, the younger generation of workers are demanding a more inclusive work environment. Employers have begun to turn to laws for more direction on maintaining a compliant and diverse workforce.

In February 2021, the House passed the Equality Act. The act codified the Bostock ruling by specifically including sexual orientation and gender identity in U.S. civil rights laws. It also updated sections of the Civil Rights Act that cover federally-funded programs and public accommodations to include prohibitions on sex discrimination.

Some companies are doing more to support new laws as they publicly oppose bills that would restrict the rights of transgender individuals. Organizations seek to curtail challenges with recruitment and retention by ensuring their companies are inclusive and inviting.

6.5 Disabilities and ADA

Leaders and managers in many companies are still learning about compliance requirements, laws, and other acts to help promote best practices for hiring job requirements. Companies have historically run into issues concerning disabled individuals and their hiring practices or accommodation requirements. In section 2.2. under Physical and Mental Abilities, we learned that a **physical disability** is a condition that negatively affects a person's stamina, dexterity, mobility, or physical capacity. There is a wide range of physical disabilities and each can vary in intensity, severity, or lasting effect over time.

The Americans with Disabilities Act (ADA) of 1990 is a far-reaching law that protects individuals with disabilities from workplace discrimination. The act prohibits discrimination based on disability in all employment practices, including application processes, hiring, terminations, promotions, compensation, and training. Although the ADA has been a prevailing force for fairness in the workplace, personal biases and perceptions still dominate many decision-making authorities. The presumption that an individual lacks the physical capability to perform a job can prevent hiring the best talent.

Although many business leaders are familiar with the term ADA and its protections, diversity literacy among decision-makers can help remove biases, stereotypes, and stigmas associated with disabled persons and the ability to work. Enhancing literacy and knowledge about ways to work, desire to work, and ability to work are ways that companies can begin to develop their culture internally.

Figure 6.2

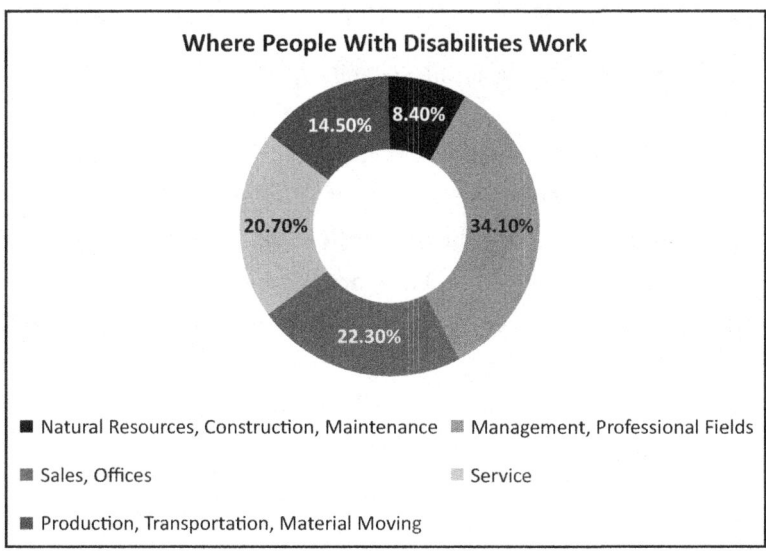

HR Magazine, vol. 65, no. 2, Summer 2020

Reflection – Disabilities and ADA

1. Recall the Superman example from earlier in the text that discussed identity. Consider an individual who attends a job interview while in a wheelchair. What are some assumptions the interviewer(s) may have?

2. What should interviewers do to avoid biases, assumptions, and prejudices concerning presumed disability?

3. Consider a woman who is presumably pregnant. If she attends an interview, what are some ways an interviewer may discriminate or show bias against her?

4. How does ADA help protect individuals who are actually physically disabled rather than only presumed disabled?

5. Research. What are some things that companies can do to comply with ADA regulations?

"Less than 14% of workers with disabilities seek special equipment or other workplace modifications, and when they do, the cost is usually negligible. Here are the most common changes sought and the percentage of workers seeking each one." – HR Magazine, Summer 2020.

Figure 6.3

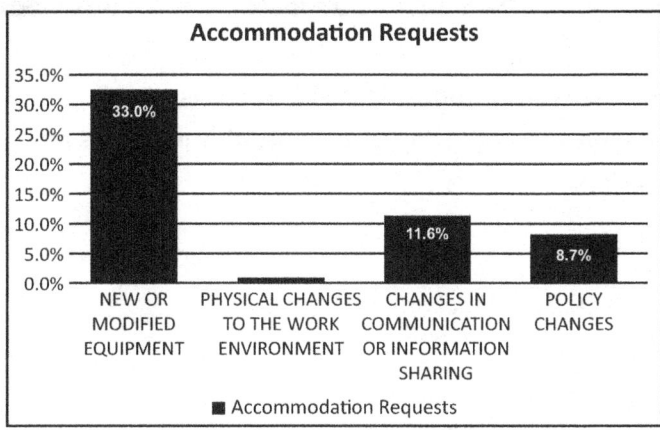

HR Magazine, vol. 65, no. 2, Summer 2020

Quiz

1. Select the word or phrase that best represents the following definition: A complex system of racial hierarchies and inequities.

    a. Racism

    b. Interpersonal racism

    c. Institutional racism

    d. Internalized racism

    e. Organizational culture

2. Select the word or phrase that best represents the following definition: Usually categorized as male or female and most often based on biological features.

    a. Sex

    b. Gender

    c. Gender identity

    d. Gender expression

3. Gloria was born with male biological reproductive organs. At birth, she was given the name George. Gloria has a mustache and dresses in traditionally masculine attire. She works as a construction worker and always uses the men's restroom when she works inside of various facilities. She requests that her coworkers and others refer to her as Gloria and use the pronouns, "she" and "her" when referring to her. Gloria's request and identifying characteristics, including her name may generally be considered which of the following?

    a. A physical or mental disability

    b. A stereotype about sex

    c. Gender identity and expression

    d. A stereotype about awareness

4. Select the word or phrase that best represents the following definition: A term that encompasses all people who experience and identify with a different gender than that of their assigned sex at birth.

    a. Agender

    b. Transgender

    c. Cisgender

    d. Bigender

5. **Which of the following describes the Americans with Disabilities Act (ADA) of 1990 do? Select all that apply.**

   a. Prohibits discrimination based on disability in all employment practices

   b. Protects individuals with disabilities from workplace discrimination

   c. Requires companies to implement DE&I programs if they have more than 20 employees.

   d. All of the Above

   e. None of the Above

Answers	1 – a	2 – a	3 – c	4 – b	5 – a, b

 *Detailed Explanation to the above questions can be downloaded from the* **Online Resources** *section of this book on* **www.vibrantpublishers.com**

Chapter Summary

- Diversity literacy can be complex as people continue to expound diversity in identity.

- The workplace focuses on specific terms and identifiers to ensure legal compliance, social responsibility, cultural awareness, and other aspects of building vibrant teams and cultures.

- Race is also an ideology historically used as a basis for domination, bias, and discrimination. It still has a prominent and lingering influence on social climates, identity formation, and self-perception, including behaviors and perceptions in the workplace.

- Social responses within specific cultures may dictate how a person's race is perceived.

- There are rules and laws pertaining to age and hiring practices.

- Companies that do not understand or value the personal differences in religion may find it challenging to create diverse, inclusive, and progressive cultures.

- Gender identity and expression have presented enlightening perspectives that require companies to reevaluate policies and their historical correlations between a person's identity, sex, gender, and work requirements.

- A person's gender identity is how they identify themselves.

- Gender identity is broad and permits a spectrum of identifying characteristics.

- Gender expression and presentation involve mannerisms, clothing choices, name selection, pronoun choices, and other outward ways a person expresses themselves.

- The gender identity spectrum includes LGBTQIA+ and other identities.

- The Americans with Disabilities Act (ADA) of 1990 is a far-reaching law that protects individuals with disabilities from workplace discrimination.

Chapter 7

Leveraging Talent

Chapter seven discusses methods and concepts for leveraging talent. It explains how organizations use assessment tools to determine best fits for cultures, teams, and groups. The chapter focuses on several common tools, including Myers Briggs Type Indicator (MBTI), the 9-Box grid, DiSC Assessment, the Predictive Index (PI), Keirsey Temperament Sorter (KTS), and Clifton's StrengthsFinder. Each assessment tool is explained to provide details about how the tool is utilized. Chapter seven also introduces the concept of 'flow state' and provides examples of how employers can identify, nurture, and leverage the talent employees exude when in the state. The chapter offers short reflection study questions to provoke progressive thought concerning flow state. Emotional Intelligence (EQ) is revisited as a type of diversity that employers and managers can leverage to form more dynamic cultures. The chapter also provides readers with precautions regarding top performers and recommends soft skills as an option for recruitment diversity. Non-traditional talent pools are identified along with a few data points concerning why the talent should be explored.

> Primary learning objectives should include the reader's understanding of the following:
>
> - Definition of key terms: upskilling, flow (or flow state), soft skills
> - Identify various types of performance, behavior, or other employee assessments
> - Recognize disadvantages of various assessment tools
> - Understand the ways through which employers can leverage diverse talent
> - Identify the ways through which companies can nurture flow state
> - Determine how the flow state is identified, nurtured, and leveraged
> - Identify non-traditional talent pools and other types of talent diversity that can be leveraged

Several aspects of an organization's overall success can be attributed to employee productivity. When employees bring their diverse skills, identities, and attributes to work, they provide the company with an arsenal of tools that propel it toward success. An employee's talent is what drives their work performance. Some talents are utilized individually, while others are strategically woven into teams, groups, and other dynamics for even greater efficiencies. The objective is to determine how to leverage the diverse skills and abilities of each worker to maintain productivity and efficiency in the work environment.

Employers often make decisions that serve the best interest of the organization and its employees. A part of their decision-making includes nurturing recruitment, cultivating a diverse work environment, building organizational culture, and creating policies that impact employees positively. Making good decisions in these areas is critical to unveiling everything an employee wants to offer to their role. Recall earlier chapters that reference employee sentiments about their identity, value, and sense of belonging at work. When employees feel valued and understood, they are more likely to deliver better work outputs and performance. This chapter examines ways to discover and harness employee talent to maintain robust and productive cultures.

Diversity, equity, and inclusion require employers to look at various levels of the organization to determine where they can incorporate the most effective policies and practices. Although some companies embrace diversity in hiring, many businesses integrate more diversity in their entry-level positions than in their upper or executive-level roles. This tendency can lead to additional challenges due to a lack of diversity in upper-level roles. To address this type of circumstance, employers can engage in upskilling to diversify their talent pool and help employees obtain higher-paying jobs. **Upskilling** is providing employees with more advanced skills through additional education, training, and development. According to Chandler Macleod Group, "Workers who upskill are likely to exhibit stronger problem-solving abilities, a higher level of productivity, and a better performance overall."

There are several other ways to discover and leverage employee talent. Some organizations and human resources departments devise strategic performance and talent management plans. They create and utilize different resources to expose talent and to train and develop employees. This explores resources and methods associated with leveraging talent, including using employee assessment tools, employee flow, cultivating emotional intelligence (EQ), and recognizing top performers.

7.1 Assessment Tools

Organizations that plan to succeed in the industry must secure the best talent. Leaders, executives, and managers often attend seminars and workshops focusing on how to build effective teams and drive results. Employee diversity and individual contributions in the workplace are critical to achieving results. Companies can discover and leverage employee diversity using various assessments highlighting skills, communication style, work style, personality traits, and other characteristics. The assessments are designed to identify individuals who are the best fit for a role or the company. The goal is to harness the best talent by tapping into skill diversity to maximize performance. Different types of assessments can be used for recruiting, team-building, performance management, talent management, behavior assessments, and more.

There are several widely accepted and utilized assessment tools for tapping into employee performance, potential, and traits. Innovative and progressive leaders who endeavor to understand employees better use specific tools to assess employee behavior within work cultures. They rationalize talent acquisition and talent management efforts using metrics, data, and statistics.

Some common behavior assessment tools include Myers Briggs Type Indicator (MBTI), DiSC, The Predictive Index (PI), Keirsey Temperament Sorter (KTS), and Clifton StrengthFinder. Each assessment is distinct from the other. However, they all share a common foundation in psychology that seeks to identify predictive behaviors based on categorizing characteristics, behaviors, and feelings. The assessments provide a guideline with ranges, ratings, boxes, continuums, and deviations from a clinical sense of how desired behavior should look.

Concerns with Assessment Tools

Although there are various tools, resources, and methods for assessing talent and skill diversity, when companies encounter a distinctly unique individual and apply a standard or typical assessment tool, they may receive common results or results that do not seem to fit the mold. This phenomenon can lead to the opposite of building a diverse culture. Employers may select candidates who continually meet the mark for the assessments yet fail to build a more diverse and balanced team.

Leveraging talent requires choosing assessments and combining them with other methodologies or resources to produce valid, reliable, and comparative data focusing on leveraging the strengths of an entire team. Employee morale can suffer when employers fail to apply assessments appropriately. The well-structured definitions, ranges, and continuums of what is normal or desired versus what is not lead directly to diversity and inclusion pitfalls.

Reflection – Leveraging Talent

1. What happens when the desired or expected employee behavior does not fall perfectly into a box or continuum for the job's suggested perfect match?

2. Consider how people are diverse. Should potential employees or current employees be overlooked as viable candidates for a position or team based on assessment tools? Why or why not?

3. How can companies leverage an individual's maximum capabilities in a role?

7.1.1 "9-Box"

Some Human Resources departments use an employee assessment tool called a 9-Box grid to craft employee development and succession plans. The **9-Box** grid or matrix is a visual tool to assess employees based on current performance and future potential. Organizations rely on this tool and others to determine potential employee success. The 9-Box grid is completed by placing employees (names) in a three-by-three matrix that has different boxes associated with the grid's performance and potential dimensions. It shows on the x-axis how an employee is currently performing, and on the y-axis, their likely future potential. A variation of the grid positions employees based on goals employees have already achieved and how they achieved them. The dimensions are different, thus yielding different outputs. Typically, 9-Box assessments produce results showing the top or highly sought-after employees in the upper right box and the lesser performing ones in the lower left.

Although the 9-Box assessment indicates how diversity can be leveraged within the company, there are both advantages and disadvantages to the method. Desirably, 9-Box assessments reinforce the concept that employee value is multidimensional. Recall that employees' identity is multifaceted. They also have various skills and talents that may not be easily categorized and placed in a box conclusively.

An individual's productivity and success may rely on different environments, levels of training, or other factors. For example, a high-performing software developer who primarily works as an individual contributor may not necessarily excel in a role that requires people management skills. If the individual were offered a promotion based on exceptional work performance, employers might find that the employee is not as successful in the promotional role. Promotions are often the result of high-performing individual contributors. However, the transition from one role to the next includes different skills, talents, and abilities. A 9-Box assessment does not inherently determine future potential from one role to the next.

A disadvantage of the assessment is that it can produce inaccurate measurements, raising concerns about measuring employee potential. The method is also susceptible to bias, which can promote employee labeling or stigmas. Subsequently, 9-Box assessments can also create confusion, tension, and discord within the work environment. To avoid stigmas or biases about employees and their ranking on the grid, companies should consider using the tool as part of a more in-depth evaluation process and incorporate other relevant assessments for a more complete picture of employee suitability.

7.1.2 DiSC Assessment

The DiSC Assessment is a familiar tool that companies use to evaluate behavior, based on four different personality traits. It suggests predictive behaviors based on a psychological foundation that attempts first to define normalcy. DiSC is an acronym that measures dominance, influence, steadiness, and conscientiousness. It assesses a person's responses and categorizes them to determine how much of their behavior is characterized by each area.

7.1.3 Myers Briggs Type Indicator (MBTI)

Myers Briggs Type Indicator (MBTI) measures four scales to differentiate how people view the world. The indicator is heavily based on psychological theories that assume people have preferences that guide their motivation and situational predictability. MBTI measures extroversion and introversion and preferences that are either perceiving or judging (way of doing things) and their preference for decision making (thinking or feeling).

7.1.4 Keirsey Temperament Sorter (KTS)

The Keirsey Temperament Sorter measures temperaments and focuses on four areas: artisan, guardian, idealist, and rational. It is further distinguished by sixteen personality types that subscribe heavily to the MBTI types. KTS is a self-assessed personality questionnaire that helps people understand themselves and others better.

7.1.5 Clifton StrengthsFinder

The StrengthFinder, a tool, assesses the areas in which individuals should build strength. It measures thought patterns, feelings, and behaviors and has an underlying foundation in psychology. The tool was designed for use in a developmental context.

7.1.6 Personal Strengths Inventory (PSI)

Personal Strengths Inventory (PSI) uses comparison or comparative data to focus on what is right about people instead of focusing on weaknesses and limitations. The tool converts the complexities into simple everyday language that does not require certification to use or interpret the results. PSI embraces diversity and identifies strengths, and strategically places them on both ends of a continuum so that an individual's normal is the appropriate starting point to apply comparative strengths.

7.1.7 Predictive Index Behavioral Assessment (PI)

The PI Behavioral Assessment measures an individual's motivating drives and needs. The tool is designed to produce predictive information that determines workplace behavior. It focuses on four key factors: dominance, extraversion, patience, and formality.

7.2 Flow

Companies that genuinely embrace diversity and inclusion extend an appreciation, respect, and value beyond invitations to join an organization, group, or team. They demonstrate their commitment to inclusion by valuing the unique and diverse talents individuals bring to the workplace. When employees express their professional and creative talents, they often do so in controlled environments, like the workplace. Sometimes controlled environments can present obstacles to productivity, creativity, or best performance. Companies that understand the underlying current of identity, diversity, and behaviors of diverse individuals will leverage them by nurturing a worker's flow state.

In 1975, psychologist Mihály Csíkszentmihályi introduced the term flow state, but the concept has deeper roots that have existed for thousands of years known by many other names. Flow has also been referred to as being 'in the zone.' **Flow** is a mental state in which a person carrying out some activity is fully immersed in a feeling of energized focus, full involvement, and enjoyment in the process of the activity.

The flow state has been used interchangeably with the term hyperfocus. However, the two terms and concepts are not the same. When a person is in their flow, they are engrossed in an activity that transforms their sense of time. The state typically involves deep focus that allows the person to accomplish tasks and is viewed positively. Conversely, hyperfocus more often has a negative connotation that can cause individuals to appear unfocused. For example, hyperfocus has been tied to activities like playing video games. Spending an excessive amount of time on an activity while becoming satisfyingly captivated by one aspect of an assignment or task to the detriment of the overall assignment.

Allowing individuals to work in highly productive manners by embracing their intuitive work behavior requires embracing the complex structure of what makes individuals uniquely diverse and respecting those attributes. The saying, "Time flies when you are having fun," can be true for work. When an employee's mind has formed a deep connection with an activity or function, they can become highly engaged and move into the mental state of high energy and focus that helps them become ultra-productive while having fun.

Each individual is different. Leveraging talents through heightened experiences related to employees' flow may allow work to feel more effortless. When work feels like fun or feels easier, employees are likely to be more productive, thus, targeting the bottom line for the company.

Understanding flow is essential to providing the environments that cultivate it. Because the flow state varies from one person to the next, organizations have to build a culture that is not only inclusive, but that is adaptable so that employees can feel comfortable, welcome, and nurtured. Diversity makes these tasks daunting. The key is to respect and value diversity.

If one employee reaches a flow state by listening to music while they work, yet another person must have as much quietness as possible, companies can try to establish a culture that works for both. In some cases, it may be permissible for employees to wear personal earbuds to listen to music that does not disturb others. Sometimes décor, images, and sounds help with flow. For instance, some people may feel more Zen when surrounded by flowers or the subtle sound of running water. If feasible, allowing workers to decorate their personal and immediate workspaces with décor that is not against company policy may be an option to foster these types of environments.

Some managers may notice that there are specific times of day that certain employees work most efficiently. Employees may realize that specific projects or assignments feel effortless to perform and quickly lead to high productivity. Both employers and employees can pay closer attention to the times or occasions when employees appear to be more productive or creative. Blocking out times or assigning projects could result in the best utilization of the diversity individuals bring to the workplace based on the talent they can exude while in their flow state.

Reflection – Flow

1. What are some professions where employees have been known to be in their flow or 'the zone'?

2. What are some things that employers can do to help employees reach their flow state?

3. How can companies address various flow states of individuals within a company?

4. What type of policies could be written to address the flow state? (Hint: Consider flexible work hours or remote work policies)

7.3 Cultivate Emotional Intelligence

Recall from Section 2.12.1 that EQ represents the ability to identify and manage, evaluate, control, and express one's emotions and the emotions of others. It demonstrates the ability to achieve success at work and identifies leaders, good team players, and people who best work by themselves. Employers are attracted to an employee's emotional intelligence and how it can be controlled. To leverage this aspect of an individual's diversity and identity, companies must be aware of what employees think and determine how their emotions and thoughts ultimately impact their performance.

Controlling employee emotions is not an easy task. The task should focus on understanding emotions and utilizing the information to achieve company-related objectives. Employees may conceal emotions or even alter them based on various factors. These deviations can result in poor communication, tense work environments, underperformance, and other undesirable outcomes.

Cultivating emotional intelligence is not a task that should be taken lightly or by individuals who are not qualified to do so. Actions that are abrasive, abusive, or that invade privacy can be highly inappropriate for any professional. Employers who want to nurture talents by tapping into EQ should ensure they have the appropriate staff or individuals who possess the psychological prowess to manage such diversity.

7.4 Top Performers

Top performers can be identified in many ways. Talent management and performance management are primary functions that help determine where talent, skills, and abilities are most abundant. Top performers are valuable assets to most companies. However, they must be managed carefully to avoid biases and favoritism that may arise due to encouraging productivity. Failing to address behavioral or compliance issues, time management, or other aspects of performance by top performers can lead to organizational culture demise.

When employers distinguish between top performers and others, it can ignite tensions in the work environment. If there are noticeable diversity elements such as race, age, gender, or other factors where some employees believe favoritism is being shown, employers subject themselves to lawsuits, culture issues, and risks to bottom-line profits.

To leverage the talents and skills of top performers, managers should be careful to document performance and goal achievements in a structured manner that is easily comparable to other individuals. Performance management systems can help create and maintain adequate documentation that evidences rationale for rewarding top performers. Employers should seek to find and nurture soft skills like time management, reliability, critical thinking as well as traditionally sought-after technical skills. The highly-transferable soft skills can be applied to almost any job. Therefore, this diversity can be leveraged when it is recognized, sought after, and encouraged.

In an article by Kate Rockwood called the Hard Facts About Soft Skills (HR Magazine Summer 2021), she says, "Being gifted at performing the technical aspects of a job can take an employee only so far. To become a stellar employee or an admired leader requires an arsenal of skills that are harder to measure but critical to success. Dubbed **soft skills**, they are behaviors, personality traits, and work habits, such as collaboration, critical thinking, perseverance, and communication that help people prosper at work."

A survey of 3,100 recruiters from the US, Canada, the UK, Germany, Italy, France, the Netherlands, and Sweden revealed the most in-demand soft skills:

Figure 7.1

HR Magazine, vol. 66, no. 2, Summer 2021

Figure 7.2

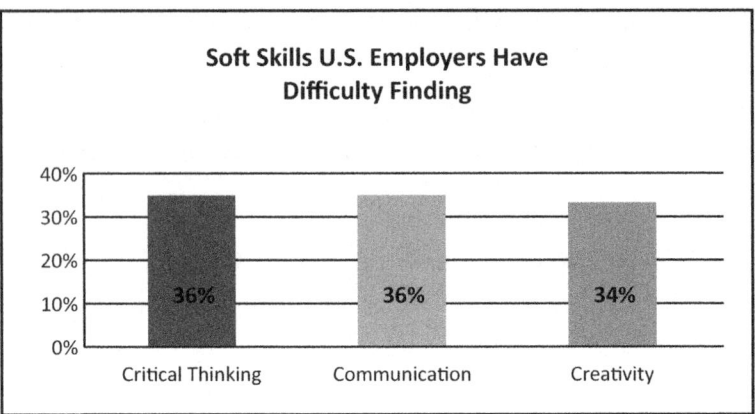

HR Magazine, vol. 66, no. 2, Summer 2021

7.5 Nontraditional Talent Pools

Most companies who have determined effective ways to attract, develop and retain talent using DE&I initiatives are familiar with accessing various talent pools. Organizations typically embrace diversity elements such as race and gender. However, some diverse talent may have been less utilized or undervalued. These nontraditional talent pools include:

- Disabled workers
- Veterans
- Aging workers
- Formerly incarcerated individuals or persons with criminal records

Although these groups may have been overlooked traditionally, they still present opportunities and options to secure highly-skilled and competent talent. Diversifying the organizational culture to include these groups will enhance diversity, equity, and inclusion efforts.

According to the source, Unlocking the Potential of the Veteran Workforce. SHRM, 2020 retrieved from the Fall 2021 edition of HR Magazine:

- 65% of veterans have some college education or higher, making them more educated than their civilian peers.

- 57% of veterans stay at their jobs longer than the median tenure of 2.5 years (for subsequent roles after their first job following active duty).

- 68% of employers report that veterans perform "better than" or "much better than" their civilian peers.

Quiz

1. Select the word or phrase that best represents the following definition: Providing employees with additional training, development and education to help them attain advanced skills.

    a. Leveraging talent

    b. Assessing talent

    c. Talent development

    d. Facilitating flow

    e. Upskilling

2. Silas is the SVP of Talent at his company. He believes strongly in using various assessment tools like MBTI, KTS, and DISC to evaluate the suitability of individuals for positions within the organization. Silas knows that assessment tools can be problematic when they are not used correctly. Which of the following is a potential concern for companies that use assessment tools?

    a. Recruiting talent that the company cannot figure out how to leverage

    b. Recruiting talent that does not believe in assessment tools and that challenges results

    c. Recruiting talent that is too diverse to fit the company culture

    d. Recruiting talent that continually fits the same mold and that results in a less diverse culture

3. Chelsea is a content writer for a large company. She primarily writes blogs about different current events. Chelsea has never missed a deadline for her work and always delivers content with great quality. Her supervisor does not like for her to work after 7PM and always tells her she will feel better if she goes home to rest. However, Chelsea disagrees and tries to convince her supervisor that she is able to produce her best work after 7PM. What is Chelsea most likely experiencing when she prefers to work after 7PM?

    a. Enhanced emotional intelligence

    b. A desire to work from home

    c. Her flow state

    d. A behavioral side-effect for being a top performer

4. Which of the following is not generally considered a non-traditional talent pool?

    a. Formerly incarcerated persons

    b. Veterans

    c. College graduates

    d. Aging workers

5. Many companies seek talent with which of the following soft skills?

   a. Teamwork and Flexibility

   b. Critical Thinking and Problem Solving

   c. Dependability and Communication

   d. A and B

   e. All of the Above

| Answers | 1 – e | 2 – d | 3 – c | 4 – c | 5 – e |

Detailed Explanation to the above questions can be downloaded from the **Online Resources** *section of this book on* **www.vibrantpublishers.com**

Chapter Summary

- Companies should determine how to leverage the diverse skills and abilities of each worker to maintain productivity and efficiency in the work environment.

- Upskilling is providing employees with more advanced skills through additional education, training, and development.

- Companies can discover and leverage employee diversity using various assessments highlighting skills, communication style, work style, personality traits, and other characteristics.

- Some common behavior, performance, or other assessment tools include Myers Briggs Type Indicator (MBTI), DiSC Assessment, The Predictive Index (PI), Keirsey Temperament Sorter (KTS), and Clifton StrengthsFinder.

- The 9-Box grid is a tool to assess employees based on current performance and future potential.

- Flow is a mental state in which a person carrying out some activity is fully immersed in a feeling of energized focus, full involvement, and enjoyment in the process of the activity.

- Cultivating emotional intelligence should be done by qualified individuals.

- ◆ To leverage the talents and skills of top performers, managers should be careful to document performance and goal achievements in a structured manner that is easily comparable to other individuals.

- ◆ Soft skills are behaviors, personality traits, and work habits, such as collaboration, critical thinking, perseverance, and communication that help people prosper at work.

- ◆ Diversifying the organizational culture to include non-traditional talent pools will enhance diversity, equity, and inclusion efforts.

Chapter **8**

Laws, Practices, and Compliance

Chapter eight explains how employment laws, practices, and business compliance affect diversity, equity, and inclusion in the workplace. Various laws have impacted how companies recruit and retain employees. The chapter outlines several laws and addresses legal and other ramifications for failure to comply with them. The distinction between laws and practices and how they are applied within the work environment is noted, and includes a focus on valuing diversity. The chapter informs readers of certain DE&I responsibilities that an employer has or should assume.

Primary learning objectives should include the reader's understanding of the following:

- Definition of key terms: compliance, equal employment opportunity (EEO) policy and qualified individual

- Identify various laws or legislation that has been enacted to promote fairness in diversity

- Understand the difference between a law and an employment practice

- Differentiate between legal requirements under EEO and valuing diversity as a practice

- Identify some responsibilities that employers have to address DE&I issues within a company

Unconscious biases, microaggressions, harassment, discrimination, and other acts that cause emotional, psychological, or physical harm to individuals in the workplace all have lasting effects. Uncomfortable or toxic environments lead to decreased productivity, individual morale issues, organizational culture issues, and more. Generally, when employees become the target of attacks related to their identity, the organization is subject to assuming some accountability. Employee safety within the walls or work environment is essential and does not allow room for individuals to perform harmful acts against each other without some form of recourse. Not all acts are intentional. Recall unconscious biases and microaggressions and how they manifest in the workplace. However, even when acts targeting someone's diversity or identity are not intentional, they can be harmful, unfair, distasteful, or unlawful. Companies have a responsibility to their employees to provide solutions for situations that arise due to diversity challenges.

The world and work environments have continually become more diverse. As they continue to develop, employers must diligently recognize toxic cultures where diversity issues are not well-managed. Once an employer is aware of situations and suffering cultures, they must attempt to address challenges with solutions that work on behalf of the employees, the company, the culture, and even the perpetrators. Sometimes, the solutions are in the form of training. Other solutions may include policy revisions or implementation. There are several practices, laws, and compliance requirements that are designed to assist organizations with building and maintaining strong cultures that evade diversity challenges. The effort to enforce practices and laws that help companies begins with conversations.

8.1 Legal Compliance

Generally, companies comply with legal and regulatory requirements as a way to evade punishment. However, many organizations are also eager to adhere to requirements to demonstrate their commitment to the growth and development of the organization and its culture. When companies follow laws that have been put in place regarding hiring, terminations, and other aspects of employment, they protect the organization and its employees from undesirable consequences. It is more beneficial to develop policies and create practices that align with regulatory and legal compliance requirements than to suffer the backlash due to nonexistent policies or unacceptable practices.

Compliance is the adherence to the rules and policies governing the management system or approach of an organization in a particular jurisdiction. Human Resources departments are often tasked with ensuring compliance with rules, policies, and employment-related laws that affect employees. However, it is the entire organization's responsibility to create a culture and environment free from actions and behaviors that compromise employee safety, security, and comfortability with the environment.

Compliance can:

- Help prevent or eliminate legal charges
- Preserve organizational integrity, reputation, and the brand
- Prevent the loss of customers or clients
- Encourage employee retention
- Promote employee loyalty, commitment, and engagement

8.2 Laws vs. Practices

Policies and practices that protect employees, like anti-harassment and anti-discrimination policies, help build higher levels of trust among business partners, employees, and clients. When a company shows its commitment to success, clients are reassured that the organization can maintain profitability.

The earlier chapters introduced concepts about diversity in hiring, promotions, termination, and other employment aspects. Many of the practices that companies follow to attract, develop and retain employees are outlined in processes. Supervisors and managers follow the processes to establish consistency. When organizations align their employment practices with laws, they are seeking to avoid punishments but also to establish fairness. They can explore diversity, equity, and inclusion in a manner that is more shielded from biases, favoritism, and prejudices. Laws provide a guide for achieving desirable DE&I results, and well-aligned practices help companies follow the guide.

Employers that implement and promote strong **equal employment opportunity (EEO) policy** throughout the company are both complying with laws and establishing sound practices. Promoting compliance with EEO laws and corresponding company policies reassures employees that they have some form of protection against injustices related to diversity issues. Strong policies provide a recourse for employees who are discriminated against and set clear standards and expectations that employers have for their employees.

Early nondiscrimination laws, such as Title VII of the Civil Rights Act of 1964, were developed on the coattail of gradually emerging diversity and inclusion challenges. As diversity became more prevalent in the workplace, it became increasingly important that laws continued to evolve or be created to strengthen protection for diverse differences like race, color, sex, disability, age, military status, national origin, and religion.

Diversity in the workplace is not confined to the characteristics and status the law has currently codified. Instead, the work environment includes differences attributed to many other factors. Throughout the last seven decades, various laws have been enacted that prevent unfair employment practices. The federal government and states have passed legislation to address and prevent unfair or unlawful employment practices. Most of the laws related to unemployment practices address some element of unfairness related to diversity, equity, or inclusion in the workplace. Some of the more notable laws over the past several decades that address discrimination, equity, fairness, or diversity include:

Equal Pay Act (1963)

According to the Society for Human Resources Management (SHRM), the "Equal Pay Act of 1963 is an amendment to the Fair Labor Standards Act which prohibits employers from discriminating between men and women by paying one gender more than the other for equal work on jobs the performance of which requires equal skill, effort, and responsibility, and which are performed under similar working conditions." Some employer-imposed penalties for non-compliance with the act include back pay for up to two years, or three years if the violation was willful, and liquidated damages in an amount equal to back pay.

There is a difference between practices and the law. Valuing diversity in a company and following legal requirements may look similar. However, here are some distinct differences between the two:

Table 8.1

Valuing Diversity	EEO
A Choice	The Law
Requests the appreciation and embracing of individuals based on all kinds of differences, including protected class	Requires tolerance and respect for individuals based on a protected class
Cannot be forced	Illegal to discriminate against individuals based on a protected class
Identifies what one can do and could do	Identifies what one cannot do and should not do

Figure 8.1

Employment Law by utah51, Adobe Stock File # 199775105

Title VII of the Civil Rights Act of 1964

Typically applying to employers with fifteen (15) or more employees, Title VII of the Civil Rights Act of 1964 is a federal law that prohibits employers from discriminating against employees on the basis of sex, race, color, national origin, religion, gender or pregnancy. These classes of individuals are "protected" under Title VII due to the historical unequal, unfair, unjust, and other treatment displayed toward the classes. The act prevents employers from discriminating based on any term, condition, or privilege of employment.

Age Discrimination in Employment Act (1969)

SHRM also defines and explains the Age Discrimination in Employment Act of 1967 (ADEA). According to SHRM, the act protects and prohibits discrimination against workers age 40 and over in any employment or employment-related decision. The Act applies to most employers with twenty (20) or more employees.

One of the main provisions of the ADEA is that employers, with very few exceptions, can no longer force an employee to retire. Voluntary retirements are allowed; however, particular conditions must be met to avoid violation of the Act. Penalties for ADEA non-compliance include: Employees may be awarded back pay, reinstatement, retroactive seniority, and attorney's fees. Also, liquidated damages equal to the amount of back pay may be awarded if the violation is willful.

Rehabilitation Act (1973)

The amended Rehabilitation Act of 1973 (Rehab Act) prohibits disability discrimination in programs conducted by federal agencies, in programs receiving federal financial assistance, in federal employment, and in the employment practices of federal contractors.

Americans with Disabilities Act (1990)

SHRM provides the following definition and explanation of the Americans with Disabilities Act (ADA):

As amended, "(ADA) is a federal anti-discrimination law which prohibits private employers, state and local governments, employment agencies, and labor unions from discriminating against qualified individuals with disabilities in job application procedures, hiring, firing, advancement, compensation, job training, and other terms, conditions and privileges of employment."

Employers with fifteen (15) or more employees are covered under ADA. It is designed to eliminate barriers that prevent qualified individuals with disabilities from receiving or enjoying the same employment opportunities extended to persons without disabilities.

ADA requires employers to make reasonable accommodations for disabled persons to do their jobs if their disability creates a barrier to employment opportunities.

A disability under ADA includes a person who:

- has a physical or mental impairment that substantially limits one or more major life activities;
- has a record of such an impairment; or
- is regarded as having such an impairment.

A **qualified individual** is one who, with or without reasonable accommodation, can perform the essential functions of a job."

Some other notable milestones for individuals with disabilities include:

- 1968 Architectural Barriers Act
- 1975 Individuals with Disabilities Act
- 1977 Section 504 of the Rehabilitation Act
- 1983 Job Accommodation Network
- 1996 Work Opportunity Tax Credit
- 1996 Mental Health Parity Act
- 1998 Section 508 of the Rehabilitation Act
- 1998 Workforce Investment Act
- 2001 Office of Disability Employment Policy
- 2004 Assistive Technology Act

- 2008 ADA Amendments Act
- 2010 Executive Order 13548
- 2014 Workforce Innovation and Opportunity Act

Civil Rights Act (1991)

The Civil Rights Act of 1991 amended parts of the Civil Rights Act of 1964 "to restore and strengthen civil rights laws that ban discrimination in employment, and for other purposes." The act also amended several sections in Title VII of the 1964 Civil Rights Act, and applied changes like, trial by jury and providing for damages in cases where there is intentional employment discrimination. The Civil Rights Act of 1991 did not require a fifteen-employee minimum distinction for enforcement and instead applied to all employers.

Pregnancy Discrimination Act (PDA) of 1978

An EEOC Fact Sheet provides the following information on the Pregnancy Discrimination Act: "The Pregnancy Discrimination Act (PDA) is an amendment to Title VII of the Civil Rights Act of 1964. Discrimination on the basis of pregnancy, childbirth, or related medical conditions constitutes unlawful sex discrimination under Title VII. Women affected by pregnancy or related conditions must be treated in the same manner as other applicants or employees who are similar in their ability or inability to work." Thus, pregnant women are to be treated the same as employees who are disabled. Employer policies have to be extended similarly regarding health benefits, leaves of absence, and reinstatements.

Genetic Information Nondiscrimination Act of 2008,

The **Genetic Information Nondiscrimination Act (GINA)** protects individuals against discrimination based on their genetic information in health coverage and in employment.

Affirmative Action

Recall the Chapter 4 discussion on Affirmative Action. In general, any employer who contracts with the government or who receives federal funds is required to document their affirmative action efforts, including metrics, outreach, and practices. The requirement is to demonstrate a deliberate reach to include a wider pool of qualified applicants. However, there is also a misconception about affirmative action and diversity in the workplace. Quotas have often been the basis of conversation when discussing affirmative action. However, Affirmative Action regulations have never required quotas.

8.3 Employer's DE&I Responsibilities

Employers are obligated to provide a safe work environment free from discrimination, harassment, and intimidation. Avoiding unlawful, unfair, discriminatory, and other undesirable practices within a company presents companies with a responsibility to pursue workplace diversity that includes equity, inclusion, and a sense of value for everyone.

Now, most employers demonstrate their commitment to DE&I acts required by law. EEO statements are prevalent on applications, websites, and company handbooks. Employers feel more secure when they create practices that adhere to and meet legal compliance requirements pertaining to EEO, equity, and other laws that attempt to establish fair and just treatment toward various classes or groups.

Some ways employers can demonstrate their commitment, accountability, and responsibility to employee diversity, equity, and inclusion include training, policy development, conforming to best practices, adhering to laws and legal mandates, establishing DE&I programs and initiatives, and promoting safe and open communication between employers and employees.

Although many governing laws have existed for years, as society continues to develop, so does the workplace. Employers must remain aware and invested in the changes in the law that affect employees. Legislation may pass at the state or federal level, and employers will be required to comply with changes. The laws may be related to race, gender, sex, criminal history, religion, pregnancy, or a myriad of other factors concerning a person's identity or diversity in the workplace.

Employers should be diligent in checking legislation and implementing any subsequent policies or practices that comply with the laws. Also, employers should establish the recourse it will take to address violations of policies and practices.

Quiz

1. True or False. It is illegal to discriminate against people based on a protected class?

    a. True

    b. False

2. Which law prohibits disability discrimination in programs conducted by federal agencies, programs that receive financial assistance from the federal government, and in employment practices of federal contractors?

    a. Title VII of the Civil Rights Act of 1964

    b. The Rehabilitation Act (1973)

    c. The Age Discrimination in Employment Act (1969)

    d. The Americans with Disabilities Act (1990)

3. Which employers are covered under the ADA?

    a. Employers who have an established DE&I program

    b. Employers with twenty or more employees

    c. Employers with fifteen or more employees

    d. Employers who have followed all regulations according to EEO

4. Employers are required to do all of the following except:

   a. Adhere to rules and policies set at local, state, and federal levels that affect employees

   b. Provide a safe work environment free from discrimination

   c. Create and administer a DE&I program

   d. Provide reasonable accommodation under ADA when applicable

5. Which of the following indicates primary differences between practices concerning valuing diversity and the law?

   a. EEO is a choice

   b. Valuing diversity is a law

   c. It is illegal to implement a DE&I program that does not address race

   d. Valuing diversity cannot be forced

   e. All of the Above

Answers	1 – a	2 – b	3 – c	4 – c	5 – d

*Detailed Explanation to the above questions can be downloaded from the **Online Resources** section of this book on **www.vibrantpublishers.com***

Chapter Summary

- Generally, companies comply with legal and regulatory requirements as a way to evade punishment.

- It is more beneficial to develop policies and create practices that align with regulatory and legal compliance requirements than to suffer the backlash due to nonexistent policies or unacceptable practices.

- Compliance is the adherence to the rules and policies governing the management system or approach of an organization in a particular jurisdiction.

- When organizations align their employment practices with laws, they are seeking to avoid punishments but also to establish fairness.

- Early nondiscrimination laws, such as Title VII of the Civil Rights Act of 1964, were developed on the coattail of gradually emerging diversity and inclusion challenges.

- A qualified individual is one who, with or without reasonable accommodation, can perform the essential functions of a job.

- Employers are obligated to provide a safe work environment free from discrimination, harassment, and intimidation.

This page is intentionally left blank

Chapter 9

Cultural Awareness

Chapter nine explores cultural awareness, the impact of community relations, and social movements. The chapter forms a correlation between employers' ability to form cultural awareness and its success with diversity, equity, and inclusion for its employees. Section 9.1. dives deeper to present strategies for helping individuals and organizations become more culturally aware. It visits the concept of six degrees of separation and introduces an emerging notion, three degrees of separation. Subsequent sections delve into the impact that the community, community relations, and social movements have on employees, groups, and subsequently the workplace. It outlines several current movements, their focus, or their cause. Chapter nine incorporates a brief reflection to provide readers with a practical example of how social movements have impacted decision-making in the workplace.

> Primary learning objectives should include the reader's understanding of the following:
>
> - Definition of key terms: cultural awareness, six degrees of separation, three degrees of separation, social movements
> - Distinguish various categories of movements and identify examples
> - Explain the concept of three degrees of separation as it relates to diversity and cultural awareness
> - Identify ways that cultural awareness can help organizations
> - Determine what cultural awareness involves
> - Identify ways individuals and companies can enhance cultural awareness
> - Identify some current local, national, or global movements

Many organizations fight relentlessly to craft reactive solutions to societal pressures. From movements like #MeToo and #BlackLivesMatter to the COVID-19 pandemic and even DE&I challenges that directly impact the workplace, companies realize a demand to make drastic changes. As a lack of common civility began to plague society and increase tensions, the external climates gradually affected organizations and employees. Discrimination, assault, harassment, the COVID-19 pandemic, cyber-attacks, social unrest, and more are all circumstances individuals may experience while away from or at work. As employees bring these life experiences to work, employers must recognize, respond to, and nurture the diversity in experiences that employees hold. These experiences may also be derived from individuals' work culture.

Rather than be reactive to such pressures when society demands attention, companies should instead shift to a proactive approach. To address the diversity among employees that involves social and other experiences, companies can engage more deliberately in cultural awareness. The National Center for Cultural Competence (NCCC) defines **cultural awareness** as being cognizant, observant, and conscious of similarities and differences among and between cultural groups. Culturally aware individuals understand the differences between people from other countries or backgrounds, especially their impact on behavior, attitudes, and values. Culturally aware organizations are conscious of organizational culture and how it is impacted by practices, policies, laws, and values.

Cultural awareness can help organizations:

- Acknowledge how culture shapes their employee experiences and perceptions
- Be more responsive to culturally diverse talent
- Be more sensitive and accessible as an ally or advocate
- Recognize cultural differences that occur within a multicultural environment
- Influence the perception and value that the next generation, public, and customers have about the organization

Cultural awareness involves:

- Understanding how culture and cultural diversity among individuals impacts organizations

- Being conscious of one's own culturally shaped values, beliefs, perceptions, and biases
- Recognizing individual responses to diverse cultures and reflecting on responses to determine if it is appropriate
- Engaging in substantive communication with individuals of diverse cultures

There is an unyielding need to develop unity within organizations. Leadership must take the initiative to broker divisiveness and build responsiveness in a manner that creates change. Creating such change and facilitating cultural awareness and responsiveness will promote employee engagement, satisfaction, and retention.

Social media has a prominent presence in unveiling worldwide social climates. Employees take to the platform to express their sentiments about their personal lives, but also about the work cultures they experience. Some companies have implemented rules and policies that prohibit employees from posting or engaging on the platforms when discussing work issues or work culture. However, social media has gained significance in both exposing strengths and weaknesses of companies, their employees, and company values that relate to cultural awareness. Undesirable recognition on social media or by word of mouth from dissatisfied employees can lead to a lack of trust from the community, job loss, biases, stigmatized reputations, loss of customers, and more. These outcomes negatively impact the organization's goal to establish diverse and inclusive cultures.

Because of the different cultures, backgrounds, and experiences that employees have, employers need to remain aware of employee sentiments concerning such cultures. Even without using social media platforms, employers can extend opportunities for their employees to express their concerns and perceptions. Encouraging employees to follow the company's lead in embracing various cultures can also demonstrate a commitment to awareness.

9.1 Improving Cultural Awareness

Cultural awareness is an individual endeavor and one in which organizations can engage. It is crucial for individuals to know, understand, and be aware of their personal cultural diversity and experiences and that of others.

The familiar concept of **six degrees of separation** is the notion that all people are six or fewer social connections away from each other. This means that to be the friend of a friend or acquaintance of an acquaintance, a connection between any two people can be made with a maximum of six introductions from one friend to the next. A newer concept, **three degrees of separation**, suggests that the average person is now connected by just three degrees based on a shared interest or social group that is a part of one of three main networks: family, friends, or work. Essentially, an individual or group can improve cultural awareness by merely tapping into one of the three networks and determining within the network who shares interests, perceptions, experiences, or other cultural connections with them.

Individual Cultural Awareness

Some ways individuals can enhance their own cultural awareness and commitment to diversity include:

- Attending plays, dance recitals, concerts, or other performing arts events by artists whose race, ethnicity, background, or culture differs from one's own
- Visiting museums, libraries, cultural centers, or other locations that display historical context for various cultures and groups
- Experiencing ethnic variety in food, groceries, and other shopping items by visiting specialty markets or venues
- Actively participating in a diversity and inclusion initiative
- Learning a new language
- Becoming an advocate or ally when injustices, unfairness, or inequity is evident
- Taking a test to determine if there are hidden biases or prejudices that may not have seemed evident
- Self-reflecting to determine the perception others have concerning their attitude, behavior, and values toward others
- Setting goals to build and expand authentic relationships with diverse individuals
- Establishing a high tolerance and comfort level for transparent and open communication about race, gender, status, and other diversity issues
- Practicing civility, kindness, and understanding

- Practicing equality and fairness when handling children or friends of different sexes (e.g., nurturing girls while encouraging boys to "suck it up")

Cultural Awareness in the Workplace

Organizational commitment to cultural awareness is imperative for progressive DE&I efforts. Companies can also try innovative approaches, which are similar to activities in which individuals can enhance their personal cultural awareness. Some ways to embrace diversity and expound on cultural awareness for employees within the workplace are:

- Establish and widely-promote internal procedures for employees to report harassment, discrimination, assault, and other incidents related to diversity.

- Create a robust DE&I program.

- Advocate for domestic partnership and ensure equitable policies.

- Reprimand managers and employees for failing to comply with protective policies and laws.

- Partner with schools, churches, or community centers to extend awareness of corporate cultural awareness.

- Add social justice funds to retirement and deferment investment options.

- Avoid singling out individuals of a particular race, gender, ethnicity, or group to speak on behalf of others or to address diversity issues on behalf of others who share identity with the group.

- Evaluate diversity at all levels of the organization.

- Engage in fair and equitable hiring and employment practices.

- Utilize or donate tolerance-related books, film, and other material for training purposes.

- Establish a diversity conflict resolution team or committee.

- Create a program for bilingual or multilingual individuals to work with team members or coworkers voluntarily.

- Discourage the use of divisive, abrasive, or insensitive logos, emblems, content, or material that employees may possess personally, yet be mindful of the way efforts and intentions can be coopted and used to further bigotry instead of acceptance (e.g., opposition to Black Lives Matter, coopting the intent of the movement and message).

- Encourage compliance with all legal mandates, regulations, and laws.

- Provide confidential methods for employees to express harassment, microaggressions, or other sensitive matters where employees may not feel comfortable engaging in an open procedure or process.

9.2 Community Relations and Impact on the Workplace

Ever-changing social, political, and economic cultural climates collectively affect the global community. As the world experiences progress in some areas, it regresses in others. One call to action has been for large organizations, business owners, and renowned leaders to step forward and facilitate the mending of global community relations. The unprecedented impact on businesses within a community results from a demand for cultural awareness. Individuals want to be heard, and they want their employers to take note.

As communities become more resilient, they look to build strong connections with companies, brands, and leaders who will advocate for their unique cause. Having the support of companies reaffirms intolerance for injustice and unfairness. Individuals want to experience the same respect, empowerment, and tolerance they fight for in the communities while at work. Therefore, community relations have a critical impact on the workplace as employees observe and await the response and reactions that their employers make concerning social and cultural happenings within the community.

Fostering an environment that does not shy away from tumultuous circumstances is critical to building employee trust. A culture of unity is established rather than divisiveness between the work environment and one's home life when employers weigh in on shifts in the culture.

Reflection – Cultural Awareness

An article in HR Magazine (Fall 2021) by Novid Parsi titled "Hitting the Mark" references Target's approach to DE&I. Kiera Fernandez, Target's senior vice president of talent and change and chief diversity and inclusion officer, states, "Target didn't suddenly start thinking about social justice in 2020 when protests and turmoil roiled the U.S. The company already had a robust diversity, equity, and inclusion (DE&I) strategy."

According to Ms. Fernandez, the roughly sixteen-year-old strategy took about nine years to establish the store's DE&I office, team, and capabilities. In the subsequent years, the store worked to refine its strategy, goals, metrics, and outcomes to its current state.

The article reports that amid the COVID-19 pandemic and rising racial tensions in the communities, Target's CEO, Brian Cornell, said his first reaction to watching the TV coverage of the (George) Floyd killing was to think, "That could have been one of my Target team members."

Target's response was to act and support its 400,000 workers worldwide. Leadership facilitated listening sessions, allowing marginalized groups and others to express concerns, desires, and perceptions about how the social and cultural events affected them personally. The company further committed to offering new benefits, like paid leave for vulnerable employees, transportation assistance for employees who lived in certain areas, and ultimately creating their REACH (Racial Equity Action and Change) program. REACH established specific target goals and focused on creating lasting change for the Black community.

1. What are some ways that other companies or business leaders have responded to social or cultural turmoil, demonstrating their cultural awareness or responsiveness?

Employment Law by utah51, Adobe Stock File # 199775105

9.2.1 Movements and causes

The potential impact of cultural and societal movements is substantial. Movements are demonstrations that seek to reach beyond the voices in individual communities. They can manifest at various levels and are often recognized globally. Leaders and community representatives look to employers to promote causes and support ideals. Visionary, progressive, and culturally aware organizations will establish firm responsiveness that invites the community to call on them when needed. Creating trust and dependence between organizations and the community will strengthen movements and promote awareness at various levels.

Many movements are stigmatized with misconceptions. These stigmas often have a source in racism, sexism, gender inequality, discrimination, or other harmful notions. Tapping into conversations about the external movements and how they will internally impact organizations will create an opportunity for growth and cultural development.

On the surface, not all movements or social unrest may relate to employment or the workplace. However, recall that each individual has a unique identity. Their identity is formed by physical attributes and composition of what they experience, their ethnicity, and the environments in which they live, worship, or work. Consider the psychological and mental effects that various movements within a social climate have on an individual. When an individual brings their whole and authentic self to work, they bring with them the anger, depression, and other emotions that have been triggered due to not being heard, respected, or valued in society.

Companies must be culturally aware of these movements and happenings within the society and community to appropriately address the impact on the workplace, its employees, and subsequently the organizational culture.

Social movements are the deliberate and purposeful involvement of organized groups to cause fundamental changes for a common goal. Movements can occur at the local, national, or global level. From individual towns and communities to strategic movements that travel continental lines, people find themselves amid cultural changes that demand awareness. Today's technology makes access to information and happenings concerning social, political, and other movements abundant. Many movements are fueled by the sheer number of people that can be reached at any given time around the world.

David Aberle (1966) is a sociologist who developed categories that distinguished various social movements. The categories and some examples include:

- **Reform movements** – focused on changing something specific about the social structure. (ex: The Human Rights Campaign's advocacy for Marriage Equality)

- **Revolutionary movements** – focused on changing every aspect of society (ex: The 1960s counterculture movement)

- **Religious/Redemptive movements** - "Meaning seeking" movements to provoke an individual's inner or spiritual growth (ex: Heaven's Gate)

- **Alternative movements** - focused on self-improvement and limited, specific changes to individual beliefs and behavior (ex: A macrobiotic diet)

- **Resistance movements** – focus on preventing or undoing the change to the social structure (ex: #BLM movement)

Some current social movements ranging from local to global reach include:

- Abahlali baseMjondolo (South Africa)
- Black Lives Matter
- Disability rights movement
- LGBTQ+ social movements
- Occupy Movement (Global anti-capitalist movement)
- Rastafari
- Shahbag Movement (Movement demanding trial of crimes against humanity) (Bangladesh)
- The Zeitgeist Movement (Global sustainability advocacy movement about the perceived roots of social problems.)

Nationally, gay marriage has been an issue to ignite many activist groups. Gay marriage is not only a social or cultural issue but has roots within the workplace. Employers must ensure cultural awareness to adequately address policy changes related to benefits, leaves of absence, and other workplace implications. Although the issue prompts legal response at the state level, it is still a national matter that various states and local businesses must address to ensure equity and true fairness in diversity.

Conversely, the National Organization for Marriage is an organization that funds campaigns to stop same-sex marriage. Similar to employers' need to be aware of cultural happenings for one issue and group of supporters, it must be equally aware of opposing perspectives. Organizations have to comply with shifts in the legal realm that require diversity, equity, or inclusion solutions. However, they must also be prepared to address employees, groups, activists, and others whose opinions and perspectives differ, thus promoting their commitment to diversity and hearing and respecting all voices and cultural dynamics.

Globally, some organizations are concerned with issues that could impact anyone worldwide, like sex trafficking or the use of genetically modified organisms (GMOs) in food. These issues are not conformed to a locality but could impact diverse individuals anywhere. The topics and goals for movements associated with the issues should not impede organizations from listening, trying to understand, or offering solutions if the company is inclined to take a stance.

Business leaders must embrace the voices of a frustrated workforce that merely expect to feel valued, heard, and supported in various walks of their lives, including at work. Companies with leaders who listen and subsequently act to demonstrate acceptance of diversity in values, opinions, or perceptions, are likely to be among the most progressive and sought-after employers of choice. Employers have to be savvy enough to recognize the diversity outside of its walls and remain culturally aware of personal or individual goals that may manifest as desires or demands even in the workplace.

Cultural Awareness Tools for Community Relations

Some ways to embrace diversity and expound on cultural awareness between employers and the communities within proximity of the workplace include:

- Initiating a group of volunteers who speak various languages to serve as interpreters or advocates for multilingual people in your organization and community
- Encouraging local public officials to be activists for tolerance, diversity, and acceptance (or diversity and inclusion)
- Conducting a diversity round-table to be held monthly or quarterly that involves the community and critical issues
- Hosting a multicultural event that celebrates various forms of diversity
- Soliciting the assistance of law enforcement agencies to collaborate on diversity and cultural awareness
- Conducting a disabilities awareness event with the help of local rehabilitation organizations
- Advocating for the protection of diverse individuals in the communities, extending to women, gay and lesbian people, minorities, and other groups that may be vulnerable.

Quiz

1. Which of the following best describes a revolutionary movement?

    a. Focused on changing something specific about the social structure

    b. Focused on preventing or undoing change to the social structure

    c. Focused on self-improvement and specific changes to individual beliefs

    d. Focused on changing every aspect of society

2. Movements are often:

    a. Lacking diversity

    b. Ineffective

    c. Unnecessary

    d. Stigmatized

3. How do community relations and social climates affect the workplace?

   a. Community involvement prevents companies from being productive.

   b. Communities look to companies to facilitate the mending of global community relations.

   c. Community relations ignite divisiveness between one's work life and home life.

   d. Organizations most often negatively impact community objectives when they get involved with community affairs.

4. What is the concept of three degrees of separation?

   a. Most people have an average of three family members who have worked with them in some capacity.

   b. The average person is connected to another person by either family, friends, or work.

   c. All people are six or fewer connections away from each other.

   d. The average employee has worked at three organizations or more, making them familiar with almost any industry.

5. Which is the best definition for cultural awareness?

   a. Being cognizant, observant, and conscious of similarities and differences among and between cultural groups

   b. Deliberate and purposeful involvement of organized groups to cause fundamental changes for a common goal.

   c. Being more responsive to culturally diverse talent

   d. Implemented rules and policies that prohibit employees from posting or engaging on the platforms when discussing work issues or work culture.

Answers	1 – d	2 – d	3 – b	4 – b	5 – a

Detailed Explanation to the above questions can be downloaded from the **Online Resources** *section of this book on* **www.vibrantpublishers.com**

Chapter Summary

- To address the diversity among employees that involves social and other experiences, companies can engage more deliberately in cultural awareness.

- Cultural awareness is being cognizant, observant, and conscious of similarities and differences among and between cultural groups.

- Leadership must take the initiative to broker divisiveness and build responsiveness in a manner that creates change.

- Creating such change and facilitating cultural awareness and responsiveness will promote employee engagement, satisfaction, and retention.

- Three degrees of separation suggests that the average person is now connected by just three degrees based on a shared interest or social group that is a part of one of three main networks: family, friends, or work.

- As communities become more resilient, they look to build strong connections with companies, brands, and leaders who will advocate for their unique cause. Having the support of companies reaffirms intolerance for injustice and unfairness.

- Fostering an environment that does not shy away from tumultuous circumstances is critical to building employee trust.

- ◆ Movements are demonstrations that seek to reach beyond the voices in individual communities. Social movements are the deliberate and purposeful involvement of organized groups to cause fundamental changes for a common goal.

Chapter 10

Systemic Change

Chapter ten is the final chapter of the book. It wraps up the previous topics discussed by presenting a call to action. This chapter discusses ways to approach and plan a DE&I program. This chapter also focuses on systemic change, organizational development, critical conversations, and training and development for employees. Each subtopic or concept explores goals that companies can seek to initiate systemic change for their organization. Some brief data points are presented to provide a practical view of how employers address DE&I. The chapter outlines a model for change management.

Primary learning objectives should include the reader's understanding of the following:

- Definition of key terms: systemic change, organizational development (OD), and change management
- Understand the goal of organizational development

- Identify primary challenges employers face in meeting DE&I goals
- Identify common tactics to achieve greater diversity in hiring
- Understand the steps necessary for change management
- Understand the concept of critical conversations
- Explain how training and development on DE&I issues affect a company

Cultural and social issues stemming from diversity can all affect the workplace. Various challenges have broadened the scope of what many believe is necessary to make an effectual change for the better. Rather than relying on correcting a single issue, an increasingly widespread concept is the need for systemic change. **Systemic change** refers to the holistic and fundamental change in any system, where the system is transformed. In cases where diversity issues cause detrimental damage to communities, individuals, or the workplace, the objective is to seek a change in the entire system that results in the damages. The system may be racial equality, the justice system, capitalism, or even a system of hiring practices within an organization.

Adequately addressing diversity issues in the workplace involves examining individual identity, organizational culture, talent acquisition, laws, cultural awareness, and many other factors. This text has introduced various elements of how organizations should approach understanding diversity at work. Recall that the ultimate goal is to recognize, respond to, and nurture diversity. For many organizations, these objectives may require creating a new outlook or restructuring previous systems.

Turning the dial to reach a more effective outcome requires some type of change.

10.1 Turning the Dial in the Workplace

Consider what identity and diversity means. Essentially, diversity is about differences. However, it is clear from exploring the value of diversity that being different, especially concerning individuals, does not make a person better. Different does not inherently mean better. However, better fundamentally means different. Organizations that seek something different to enhance their diversity do not necessarily receive something better when they find it. However, if organizations wish to have something better, they must absolutely seek something different. This realization is where companies must consider turning the dial.

Some organizations begin with organizational development. **Organizational Development (OD)** relies on systemically planned development and procedures to identify and solve problems within the organization. It is a planned process for change in an organization's culture through behavioral science, technology, research, and theory. The goal of OD is the betterment of an organization. This includes revamping policies, strategies, organizational culture, and more. However, each area collectively affects one of the most important aspects of any organization, its people.

Employees are the key to most company operations. They are the producers of products and crafters of service. Employees deliver their talents and skills, and in return, the company grows and develops. Pouring into employees requires all of the tactics concerning valuing diversity, equity, and inclusion previously discussed. Additionally, to enhance the nurture aspect of valuing diversity, employees require a conducive work environment, individual and group training, demonstrated appreciation, and more. Companies must deliberately attempt to try something different to achieve something better.

Taking the initiative to implement organizational development changes is an excellent first step. All plans and efforts should align with the strategic goals to avoid undesirable results. The processes to achieve desired results will vary depending on a company's overall objective. For example, some companies may already have robust training and development programs and merely need to incorporate specific topics or curricula. Other companies may not have a training and development program in place at all and may need to create one. Either way, using organizational development as a foundation, companies can create methodical processes designed to address diversity and other issues in the organization to facilitate systemic change.

According to LEVER, DE&I Report 2021 Report Highlights: The State of Diversity, Equity, and Inclusion Efforts, there are three primary challenges employers face in meeting DE&I goals. They include:

- Difficulty finding time on top of assigned work responsibilities - 44%
- Difficulty finding diverse applicants/lack of interest - 43%
- Budget restrictions – 32%

Figure 10.1

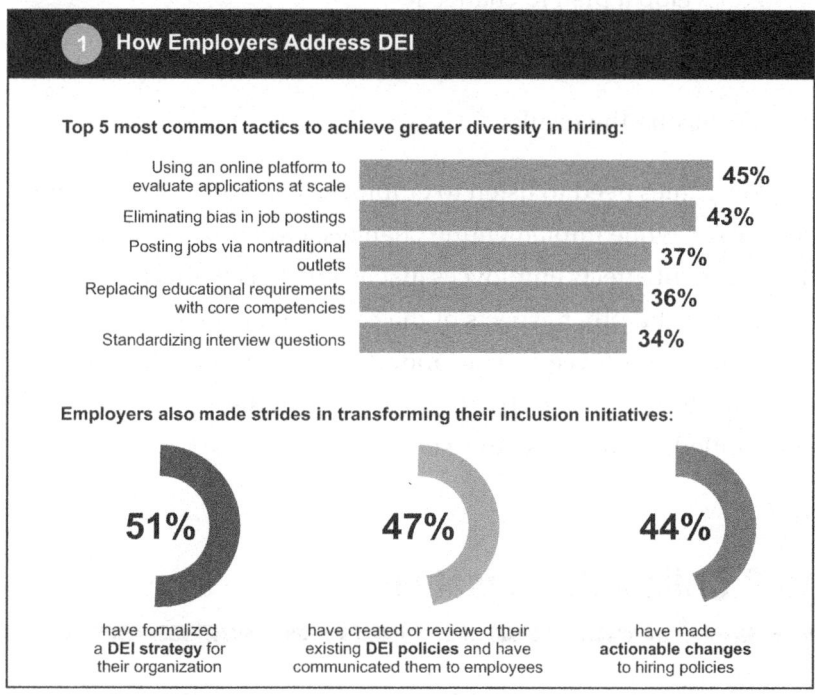

LEVER, DE&I Report, 2021 Report Highlights: The State of Diversity, Equity, and Inclusion Efforts

Organizational leaders approach situations from various perspectives. Change specifically requires situational leaders. Leaders must recognize different situations and customize their approach and response to manage change effectively. **Change Management** is the systematic approach and application of knowledge, tools, and resources to deal with change. Effective change management results in newly implemented processes and business strategies and deters adverse outcomes. Gil-Avila summarizes a model for change management in the following steps:

1. Analyze what needs to change and who is impacted
2. Develop a plan to change it
3. Execute the plan
4. Measure the results

Companies need to listen to employees and other stakeholders before and while implementing changes. Organizational development affects employees just as much as it affects operations and other aspects of the company. Failing to incorporate employee values, opinions, and concerns into the strategic design for the change may result in disapproving, disgruntled, or unsupportive staff.

10.2 Critical Conversations

As companies explore DE&I options, they have to unveil various emotions that employees and others may harbor. Conversations about race, gender, religion, age, and other elements of diversity within the work environment can be difficult. Although attempting to move in a positive direction such as organizational development, implementing change, or engaging in cultural awareness, these endeavors can create unforeseen obstacles. Employees may not be ready to have specific conversations. Managers may be unprepared to discuss topics professionally. The community may play a more prominent role in igniting or calming some issues that directly affect the workplace.

Organizations have to devise a strategic and transparent method for introducing and facilitating critical conversations, especially those often avoided. Johnny C. Taylor, Jr., SHRM-SCP, wrote in HR Magazine (Summer 2021), "Workplace bias and racial inequity bloom in the dark. If we continue to be silent-unable to speak candidly about our uncomfortable experiences and those of others-nothing will change." Mr. Taylor's sentiment is similarly shared and widespread among pioneers who realize the need for change. Difficult and critical conversations concerning diversity, equity, and inclusion in the workplace must be a practical part of any change management strategy. To achieve a deeper reflection of diversity and inclusion, systemic change must be infused with conversations that enlighten, challenge, and support leadership and decision-making.

Figure 10.2

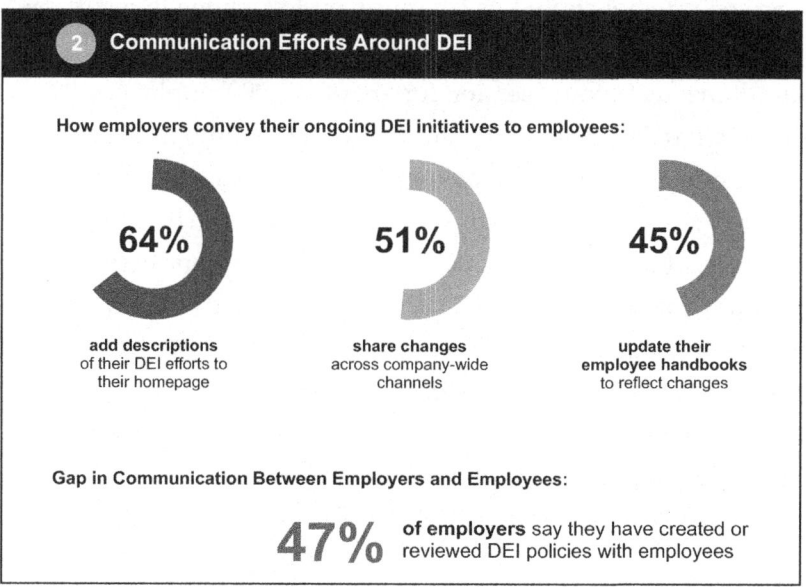

LEVER, DE&I Report 2021 Report Highlights: The State of Diversity, Equity, and Inclusion Efforts

A recent issue concerning a socially, politically, and culturally charged incident demonstrated how some large companies might respond to diversity and cultural awareness challenges. A Philadelphia Starbucks received much attention when two BLACK patrons were arrested for suspicion of trespassing. Officials reported that the two men asked to use the restroom but were denied because they had not purchased anything from the store. Subsequently, they were asked to leave. After declining to leave, the police were called, and the two men were arrested. While the police commissioner for Philadelphia defended the officers' actions, Starbucks apologized.

An apology from top leadership at the organization was not likely a final decision without also addressing difficult and critical conversations with employees, staff, and others. Starbucks demonstrated its commitment to tackling diversity and inclusion issues by closing 8,000 stores for one day to conduct a simultaneous training session for about 175,000 employees. The top-down decision to interweave conversation into its leadership discussion and the store's team of employees was a deliberate effort to create systemic change for the company. This text does not purport to know the details of any conversations between Starbucks, its employees, or leadership, yet, the demonstrative result was a culturally aware response to bias, discrimination, or cultural insensitivity. The impact of such a large organization taking a stance further prompted conversations among other employers that focus on promoting intentional inclusion.

10.3 Training and Development

An employer's commitment to DE&I does not begin and end with conveying information. Although communicating expectations and policies is essential, workplace diversity does not end with a company posting an EEO sign in the office or blurb on an employment site. Employers must also train their employees on diversity and inclusion topics. Training has to be extended to new hires to acclimate them to a culture and to also convey expectations immediately. Training should also be provided for current employees regularly and to comply with specific laws or training requirements for various industries.

Recall the discussion about unconscious biases, stereotypes, stigmas, and prejudices. These assumptions directly affect how employees are viewed and can subsequently affect how employees perform in the workplace. While employers seek to attain employees with the best talent and skills, they also hope to leverage good work performance. Enhancing performance can be facilitated when employers provide additional or necessary training and development for their workers.

Employers may assess employee performance in technical areas involving skills like engineering, weapons handling, or cooking. However, employers can also evaluate employee performance in areas that require soft skills like communication, critical thinking, and enhanced cultural awareness. Companies that help employees develop both technical and soft skills will likely experience enhanced results concerning the employee's acclimation to the organizational culture. Acclimation to a culture where DE&I is ingrained helps the employee develop naturally, yet progressively.

When DE&I issues arise in the workplace, employees that have been trained to utilize soft skills will be better equipped to engage in substantive conversation and to adapt to change in the workplace. Without appropriate training to help employees acclimate to the culture, workers eventually learn and demonstrate their progress over time. However, this gradual advance in organizational culture or development can be problematic.

Direct or immediate training helps employees develop at a faster pace. Allowing employees to adapt naturally without training can cost companies a significant amount of time and generate ineffective yields. Recall that a part of diversity is how people learn. Therefore, letting individuals adapt naturally, while providing no training, can be ineffective because some employees will not progress as fast as others, leaving the organization's health compromised.

Providing training and development on diversity and inclusion topics helps enhance employees' competence and serves the collective good of the organization. However, when an organizational development, people development, or change management effort is initiated without an adequate strategic plan, the goals will likely be compromised and produce undesirable results for individuals and the company. Subsequently, diversity, equity, and inclusion attempts suffer even greater because employees and others can lose faith in the process or potential outcome.

Training and development for employees can include several topics. The curriculum may encompass many ideas, elements, or factors of identity and diversity. Leaders must be committed to listening to employees, stakeholders, the community, and other voices that beg for a place in the diversity and inclusion conversation. Critical conversations will spark the change that most organizations seek and ultimately turn the dial toward accomplishing DE&I success within any company.

Figure 10.3

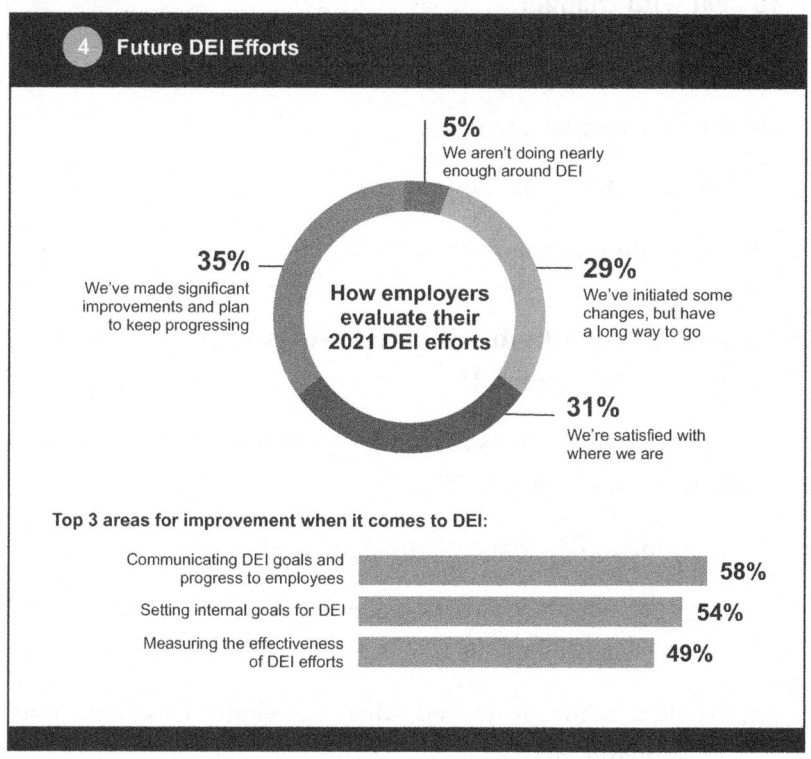

LEVER, DE&I Report   2021 Report Highlights: The State of Diversity, Equity, and Inclusion Efforts

Quiz

1. Which word or phrase is best described as the systematic approach and application of knowledge, tools, and resources to deal with change?

    a. Systemic change

    b. Change management

    c. Organizational development

    d. Diversity management

2. Which order of activities best represents an effective model for change management?

    a. Analyze what needs to change, Measure results, Develop a plan, Execute the plan

    b. Develop a plan, Execute the plan, Measure results

    c. Analyze what needs to change, Develop a plan, Execute the plan, Measure Results

    d. Analyze who is Impacted, Measure results, Develop a plan, Execute the plan

3. True or False? To address diversity issues in the work environment, companies should examine individual identity, organizational culture, talent acquisition, laws, cultural awareness, and other factors.

    a. True

    b. False

4. What is meant by engaging in critical conversations concerning workplace diversity?

    a. Conversations about diversity elements like race, gender, and age can be difficult

    b. Employees may not be ready to have specific conversations at work

    c. Managers may be unprepared to discuss some topics professionally

    d. All of the Above

    e. None of the Above

5. **How have organizations recently begun to express their commitment to DE&I in the workplace.**

    a. By reviewing case law concerning EEO and ADA compliance

    b. By separating company and business operations from community relations

    c. By implementing training and development programs that focus on DE&I.

    d. By disseminating hard copies of employee handbooks to ensure each employee has a copy.

| Answers | 1 – b | 2 – c | 3 – a | 4 – d | 5 – c |

Detailed Explanation to the above questions can be downloaded from the **Online Resources** *section of this book on* **www.vibrantpublishers.com**

Chapter Summary

- Systemic change refers to the holistic and fundamental change in any system, where the system is transformed.

- Organizational Development (OD) relies on systemically planned development and procedures to identify and solve problems within the organization.

- The goal of OD is the betterment of an organization.

- Companies must deliberately attempt to try something different to achieve something better.

- Change Management is the systematic approach and application of knowledge, tools, and resources to deal with change.

- Effective change management results in newly implemented processes and business strategies and deters adverse outcomes.

- Organizations have to devise a strategic and transparent method for introducing and facilitating critical conversations, especially those often avoided.

- Enhancing performance can be facilitated when employers provide additional or necessary training and development for their workers.

- Allowing employees to adapt naturally can cost companies a significant amount of time and generate ineffective yields.

www.vibrantpublishers.com

◆ Providing training and development on diversity and inclusion topics helps enhance employees' competence and serves the collective good of the organization.

References

Books

Noe, R., Hollenbeck, J., Gerhart, B., and Wright P. *Fundamentals of Human Resources Management:* 3rd ed. New York, New York: McGraw-Hill Irwin, 2009

Gilbert, Jaquina. *Take Time to Live: 100 Ways to Invest Your Time.* Printed by the Author, 2018

Gilbert, Jaquina. *Human Resource Management: Essentials You Always Wanted to Know.* Vibrant Publishers, 2020

Bradberry, T. and Greaves, J. *Emotional Intelligence 2.0.* Talent Smart, 2009

Gostik A. and Elton, C. *The 24-Carrot Manager.* Gibbs Smith Publisher, 2004

Godin, Seth. *Linchpin: Are You Indispensable.* ed. Softcover, Portfolio, 2011

The Arbinger Institute. *Leadership and Self-Deception: Getting out of the Box.* ed. Softcover, Berrett-Koehler Publishers, 2002

Schein, Edgar H. *The Corporate Culture Survival Guide, ed. New and Revised Edition.* Jossey- Bass, 2009

Milkovich, G., Newman, J., and Gerhart, B. *Compensation.* 11th ed. McGraw-Hill Education, 2013

Bohlander, G. and Snell, S., *Managing Human Resources*. 15th ed. South-Western Cengage   Learning, 2009

An Outline of Psychoanalysis. Freud, Sigmund. An Outline of Psychoanalysis. Translated by James Strachey. New York: W.W. Norton, 1949. 124 pp.

Magazines

Kozlowski, James. "Park Administrations Back Disability ADA Claims." *Parks & Recreation,* vol. 49, no. 4, National Recreation and Park Association, Apr. 2014, p. 26

Smith, Allen. "All Things Work: Prepare Now to Address Inappropriate Office Behavior." *HR Magazine,* vol. 66, no. 3, Fall 2021, 7 - 11

HR Magazine, vol. 65, no. 2, Summer 2020

HR Magazine, vol. 66, no. 1, Spring 2021

HR Magazine, vol. 57, no. 5, May 2012

HR Magazine, vol. 66, no. 2, Summer 2021

HR Magazine, vol. 64, no. 2, Summer 2019

HR Magazine, vol. 66, no. 3, Fall 2021

Websites

"DE&I Report: 2021 Report Highlights: The State of Diversity, Equity, and Inclusion Efforts", Lever, https://www.lever.co/wp-content/uploads/2021/08/Lever-DEI-Infographic-Aug2021.pdf

Stevens, Matt, "Starbucks C.E.O. Apologizes After Arrests of 2 Black Men", The New York Times, 15 April 2018, https://www.nytimes.com/2018/04/15/us/starbucks-philadelphia-black-men-arrest.html Accessed 12/6/21

Johnny C. Taylor, Jr., "From the CEO: Racial Injustice at Work Costs Us Billions", SHRM-SCP, https://www.shrm.org/hr-today/news/hr-magazine/summer2021/pages/racial-injustice-at-work-costs-us-billions.aspx

Caporuscio, Jessica, Pharm.D., "Everything you need to know about white fragility", Medical News Today (online magazine), 12 June 2020, https://www.medicalnewstoday.com/articles/white-fragility-definition, Accessed 10/12/21

Chappell, Bill, "Starbucks Closes More Than 8,000 Stores Today For Racial Bias Training", The Two-Way, 29 May 2018, https://www.npr.org/sections/thetwo-way/2018/05/29/615119351/starbucks-closes-more-than-8-000-stores-today-for-racial-bias-training Accessed 12/6/21

"Definition of Cultural Awareness", Collins, https://www.collinsdictionary.com/us/dictionary/english/cultural-awareness Accessed 12/3/21

Parsi, Novid, "Career Lessons from Kiera Fernandez: Helping Workers Helps", SHRM, 27 August, 2021. https://www.shrm.org/hr-today/news/hr-magazine/fall2021/pages/career-lessons-from-kiera-fernandez-helping-workers-helps-the-business.aspx Accessed 12/3/21

Narberhaus, Micha, "What is Systemic Change", Medium, 30 August, 2016, https://medium.com/virtual-teams-for-systemic-change/what-is-systemic-change-f1ae8cdf2f2a Accessed 12/5/21

Parsi, Novid, "Career Lessons from Kiera Fernandez: Helping Workers Helps", SHRM, 27 August, 2021. https://www.shrm.org/hr-today/news/hr-magazine/fall2021/pages/career-lessons-from-kiera-fernandez-helping-workers-helps-the-business.aspx Accessed 12/3/21

"MCEAP Committee on Cultural Responsiveness, Cultural Responsiveness: Definitions and Principles", 28 November 2017 revised, http://www.nysed.gov/common/nysed/files/principal-project-phase-2-mceap-definition-and-guiding-principles-for-cultural-responsiveness-and-cultural-competency.pdf, Accessed 12/3/21

"Curricula Enhancement Module Series: A project of the National Center for Cultural Competence", Georgetown University, Cultural Awareness, https://nccc.georgetown.edu/curricula/awareness/index.html, Accessed 12/3/21

"What Is Racial Equity?", Race Forward, https://www.raceforward.org/about/what-is-racial-equity-key-concepts, Accessed 11/12/21

"Age Discrimination in Employment Act of 1967", SHRM, https://www.shrm.org/hr-today/public-policy/hr-public-policy-issues/pages/agediscriminationinemploymentactof1967.aspx, Accessed 11/30/21

"Rehabilitation Act of 1973 (Rehab Act)", EARN (Employer Assistance and Resource Network on Disability Inclusion), https://askearn.org/page/the-rehabilitation-act-of-1973-rehab-act#:~:text=The%20Rehabilitation%20Act%20of%201973%2C%20as%20Amended%20(Rehab%20Act),employment%20practices%20of%20federal%20contractors, Accessed 11/30/21

"Americans With Disability Act of 1990", as amended, SHRM, https://www.shrm.org/hr-today/public-policy/hr-public-policy-issues/pages/americanswithdisabilityactof1990,asamended.aspx Accessed 11/30/21

"Types of Investigations: In the Official CHFI Study Guide (Exam 212-49), 2007 - The Civil Rights Act of 1991", Science Direct, https://www.sciencedirect.com/topics/computer-science/civil-right-act, Accessed 11/30/21

"Fact Sheet: Pregnancy Discrimination", U.S. Equal Employment Opportunity Commission (EEOC), https://www.eeoc.gov/laws/guidance/fact-sheet-pregnancy-discrimination, Accessed 11/30/21

"Genetic Information", HHS.gov (Health Information Privacy), https://www.hhs.gov/hipaa/for-professionals/special-topics/genetic-information/index.html, Accessed 11/30/21

"Americans with Disabilities Act (ADA)", SHRM, https://www.shrm.org/resourcesandtools/tools-and-samples/hr-glossary/pages/americans-with-disabilities-act-ada.aspx, Accessed 11/30/21

"The Equal Pay Act of 1963", SHRM, https://www.shrm.org/hr-today/public-policy/hr-public-policy-issues/pages/theequalpayactof1963.aspx?_ga=2.170322082.364641391.1638307263-1485016633.1638307263, Accessed 11/30/21

"Title VII of the Civil Rights Act of 1964", SHRM, https://www.shrm.org/hr-today/public-policy/hr-public-policy-issues/pages/titleviiofthecivilrightsactof1964.aspx, Accessed 11/30/21

Hunt, PhD, Stephen T., "The Case for Junking 9 Box Assessments", SAP, Accessed 11/27/21

Mandapat, Hannah, "What is a 9-box grid and why might you find it helpful?", Cezanne, 4 June 2021, https://cezannehr.com/hr-blog/2021/06/what-is-a-9-box-grid/, Accessed 11/27/21

References

Jones, Ashli L., "An Employer's Responsibility for Diversity in the Workplace", Penn State Dickinson Law, 17 February 2020, https://sites.psu.edu/entrepreneurshiplaw/2020/02/17/an-employers-responsibility-for-diversity-in-the-workplace/, Accessed 11/29/21

"DE&I Report: 2021 Report Highlights: The State of Diversity, Equity, and Inclusion Efforts", Lever, https://www.lever.co/wp-content/uploads/2021/08/Lever-DEI-Infographic-Aug2021.pdf

"Upskill Definition", Merriam-Webster, https://www.merriam-webster.com/dictionary/upskill, Accessed 11/27/21

The Annie E. Casey Foundation, "Embracing equity", Eric, https://files.eric.ed.gov/fulltext/ED555532.pdf

Deichler, Andrew, "A Sense of Belonging", SHRM, 8 May 2021, https://www.shrm.org/hr-today/news/all-things-work/Pages/a-sense-of-belonging.aspx

Recinos, Andrew, "How do you define your cultural climate", Tessiture Network, 12 March 2020, https://www.tessituranetwork.com/en/Items/Articles/Andrew-Recinos/2020/Defining-Your-Climate

"What is artificial intelligence and how is it used in the workplace?", SHRM, https://www.shrm.org/resourcesandtools/tools-and-samples/hr-qa/pages/what-is-artificial-intelligence-and-how-is-it-used-in-the-workplace.aspx, Accessed 10/28/21

"11 harmful types of unconscious bias and how to interrupt them - workplaces that work for women", Catalyst, 2 January 2020, https://www.catalyst.org/2020/01/02/interrupt-unconscious-bias/ Accessed 10/26/21

Grace, Carolyn, "A guide to U.S. sexual harrasment laws and training requirements by state", LRN Corporation, 31 August 2022, https://blog.lrn.com/latest-news/training-guide-ny-and-ca-Sexual-harassment-elearning-checklist

"Glossary of EssentialHealth Equity Terms", NCCDH, March 2022, https://nccdh.ca/glossary/entry/marginalized-populations, Accessed 10/26/21

Soule, Sarah A., Drabkin, Davina and Mackenzie, "The Stereotypes in MBA Case Studies", The Harvard Business Review, 24, June 2019, https://hbr.org/2019/06/the-stereotypes-in-mba-case-studies, Accessed 11/24/21

Stereotype, Merriam-Webster, https://www.merriam-webster.com/dictionary/stereotype, Accessed 11/24/21

"Deviance and Social Stigma", LibreTexts Social Sciences, 20 February 2021, https://socialsci.libretexts.org/bookshelves/sociology/introduction_to_sociology/book%3a_sociology_(boundless)/07%3a_deviance_social_control_and_crime/7.01%3a_deviance/7.1c%3a_deviance_and_social_stigma, Accessed 11/23/21

"Understanding and Developing Organizational Culture", SHRM, https://www.shrm.org/resourcesandtools/tools-and-samples/toolkits/pages/understandinganddevelopingorganizationalculture.aspx, Accessed 10/25/21

Association of Fitness Studio, "AFS's Guide to the Employee Handbook: Handbook template", September 2021

"Microaggression", Oxford Languages, https://languages.oup.com/google-dictionary-en/, Accessed 10/25/21

Teinaki, Vicky, "Learning about designing services for deaf / Deaf people", Medium, 13 October 2019, https://medium.com/@vickytnz/learning-about-designing-services-for-deaf-deaf-people-18cc6a7a6f91, Accessed 10/22/21

Cotruș, Andrei, Camelia Stanciu, and Alina Andreea Bulborea. "EQ vs. IQ Which Is Most Important in the Success or Failure of a Student?" Procedia - Social and Behavioral Sciences 46 (January 1, 2012): 5211–13. https://doi.org/10.1016/j.sbspro.2012.06.411

Kate T., Gauri S., Nikhilesh Jasuja,"EQ vs IQ," Diffen.com. Diffen LLC, n.d. Web. 23 Oct 2021, https://www.diffen.com/difference/EQ_vs_IQ

"Soci-economic Background", The Open University Equality and Diversity, The Open University, https://www.open.ac.uk/equality-diversity/content/socio-economic-background, Accessed 10/22/21

"Status", Merriam-Webster (online), https://www.merriam-webster.com/dictionary/status, Accessed 10/21/21

"Age Discrimination", U.S. Equal Employment Opportunity Commission, https://www.eeoc.gov/age-discrimination, Accessed 10/21/21

"Women's History in America Presented by Women's International Center", WIC Main Page, http://www.wic.org/misc/history.htm, Accessed 10/19/21

Zambon, Veronica, "What are some different types of gender identity?", Medical News Today, 5 November 2020, https://www.medicalnewstoday.com/articles/types-of-gender-identity, Accessed 10/19/21

"Does having a Y chromosome make you a man? Does lacking one make you a woman?", Accord Alliance, https://www.accordalliance.org/faqs does-having-a-y-chromosome-make-you-a-man-does-lacking-one-make-you-a-woman/, Accessed 10/19/21

"Chromosome", US National Library of Medicine – MedlinePlus, https://medlineplus.gov/ency/article/002327.htm#:~:text=two%20of%20the%20chromosomes%20(the,x%20and%201%20y%20chromosome, Accessed 10/19/21

Southern Poverty Law Center, "101 Tools For Tolerance: Simple Ideas For Promoting Equity and Celebrating Diversity," Tolerance.org, 10 March 2012, www.tolerance.org.

Satterfield, Jason M. Ph.D., "The Iceberg-Visible and Hidden Identity",University of California, San Francisco, 16 February 2017, https://www.thegreatcoursesdaily.com/visible-and-hidden-identity/ ,Accessed 9/23/21

"Tip of the Iceberg", Science Learning Hub, https://www.sciencelearn.org.nz/, Accessed 10/2/21

"Identity", Psychology Today, https://www.psychologytoday.com/us/basics/identity, Accessed 9/23/21

"What is gender? What is sex?", Canadian Institute of Health Research, https://cihr-irsc.gc.ca/e/48642.html, Accessed10/2/21"What Are the 4 Genders?", MedicineNet, https://www.medicinenet.com, Accessed 10/2/21

"Equity vs. Equality and Other Racial Justice Definitions", The Annie E. Casey Foundation, 24 August 2020, https://www.aecf.org/blog/racial-justice-definitions?gclid=CjwKCAjwz5iMBhAEEiwAMEAwGBZoF8LWUbqA5YxemMXAAXf8mZKdaylpZsLz7Jb6igVp1CIQ07Jx6BoC2dAQAvD_BwE, Accessed 11/6/21

"Equity vs. Equality: What's the Difference?", GW: Online Public Health, 5 November 2020, https://onlinepublichealth.gwu.edu/resources/equity-vs-equality/, Accessed 11/6/21

References

"Affirmative Action", Definitions from Oxford Languages, Cornell Law School: Legal Information Institute, https://www.law.cornell.edu/wex/affirmative_action, Accessed 11/6/21

"18 HR Metrics Affecting Your Organizational Health", Kazoo, https://www.kazoohr.com/resources/library/hr-metrics-that-matter, Accessed 11/6/21

"Sigmund Freud's Theories", Simply Psychology, https://www.simplypsychology.org, Accessed 10/2/21

"The Identity Element, A Definition of Identity", LinkedIn, https://www.linkedin.Com

Helgeson, Jeffrey, "American Labor, and Working-Class History", 1900–1945, Published 31 August, 2016, https://doi.org/10.1093/acrefore/9780199329175.013.330, Accessed 10/11/21

"The Historic Roots of the Middle Class", Pittsburgh Post-Gazette, 11 November 2020, https://www.post-gazette.com, Accessed 10/11/21

"Slavery in America", Jim Crow Museum, https://www.ferris.edu/htmls/news/jimcrow/timeline/slavery.htm, Accessed 10/11/21

"The First Africans in Virginia Landed in 1619. It Was a Turning Point for Slavery in American History—But Not the Beginning", Time Magazine (online version), https://time.com/5653369/august-1619-jamestown-history/, Accessed 10/11/21

"Privileges", EPIC.org, https://epic.org › privacy › privileges, Accessed 10/12/21

"5 main types of privilege", Hive Learning, https://www.hivelearning.com/site/resource/diversity-inclusion/5-main-types-of-privileges/, Accessed 10/12/21

Lee Jourdan, "Diversity and Inclusion: Talk About Privilege at Work", 2 August 2020, Accessed 10/12/21

"Privilege", Dictionary.com (website), https://www.dictionary.com/browse/privilege, Accessed 10/12/21

"DE&I Report: 2021 Report Highlights: The State of Diversity, Equity, and Inclusion Efforts", Lever, https://www.lever.co/wp-content/uploads/2021/08/Lever-DEI-Infographic-Aug2021.pdf

"White fragility", Oxford Languages, https://languages.oup.com/google-dictionary-en/, Accessed 10/12/21

Caporuscio, Jessica, Pharm.D., "Everything you need to know about white fragility", Medical News Today (online magazine), 12 June 2020, https://www.medicalnewstoday.com/articles/white-fragility-definition, Accessed 10/12/21

Taylor, Bridie, "Intersectionality 101: what is it and why is it important?", Woman Kind Worldwide, 24 November 2019, https://www.womankind.org.uk/intersectionality-101-what-is-it-and-why-is-it-important/, Accessed 10/13/21

"What is intersectionality, and what does it have to do with me?", YW Boston, 29 March 2017, https://www.ywboston.org/2017/03/what-is-intersectionality-and-what-does-it-have-to-do-with-me/, Accessed 10-13-21

"Multiculturalism", Stanford Encyclopedia of Philosophy, 24 September 2010, https://plato.stanford.edu/entries/multiculturalism/, Accessed 10/13/21

Longley, Robert. "What Is Multiculturalism? Definition, Theories, and Examples", ThoughtCo, 15 October 2020, https://www.thoughtco.com/what-is-multiculturalism-4689285, Accessed 10/13/21

"DEI Toolkit: Physical & Mental Ability", AAUW, https://www.aauw.org/resources/member/governance-tools/dei-toolkit/dimensions-of-diversity/ability/

Kass, MD, Dara. "Allies, Advocates, and Accomplices Are Critical to Diversity and Inclusion.", ACEP Now, 21 October 2019, https://www.acepnow.com/article/allies-advocates-and-accomplices-are-critical-to-diversity-and-inclusion/, Accessed 1/28/22

Saguy, Abigail C., The history of 'coming out,' from secret gay code to popular political protest", The Conversation, 10 February 2020, https://theconversation.com/the-history-of-coming-out-from-secret-gay-code-to-popular-political-Protest-129609

"Generation Alpha-Generation Alpha will lead a 100% digital world", Iberdola, Accessed 7/13/22, https://www.iberdrola.com/talent/alpha-Generation

Falcone, Paul, "Women in Leadership: Closing the Gender Pay Gap", SHRM, 1 June 2022, https://www.shrm.org/executive/resources/articles/pages/women-executives-.aspx, Accessed 7/13/22

Notes

Made in the USA
Monee, IL
28 April 2026